THE
TURNING POINT

Rebuilding Your Relationship With God

ANGELA R. CAMON

Order this book online at www.trafford.com
or email orders@trafford.com

Most Trafford titles are also available at major online book retailers.

Printed in the United States of America.

ISBN: 978-1-4907-1613-8 (sc)
ISBN: 978-1-4907-1612-1 (e)

Trafford rev. 03/05/2014

 www.trafford.com

North America & international
toll-free: 1 888 232 4444 (USA & Canada)
fax: 812 355 4082

Dedication

I DEDICATE THIS BOOK TO every born again believer who has drifted off course from God and fallen back into a life of sin. It is my prayer that you will reach a turning point in your life, have the courage to come back to Christ and start rebuilding your relationship with him.

To every person who is experiencing the pain of having a family member or friend turn their back on God, let me encourage you to keep calling their name out before God and standing in the gap for them, for our God is a God of restoration.

Acknowledgments

I GIVE ALL GLORY, PRAISE and honor to my Lord and Savior Jesus Christ. Thank you Father for giving me this awesome assignment of writing The Turning Point—Rebuilding Your Relationship With God. To my husband Carl, thanks for your love and support. You are truly a blessing!! To my four children Carl Jr., Aaron, Camille and Candace. I will forever love and cherish you. To my parents, Dr. Vickery F. Williams and the late Pauline Williams, and to my sisters and their families, Pastor Tracie Davis, Vickie Smith and Kyna Williams. I love you all so much!!! To Madine Camon, keep teaching the Word of God.

Contents

Introduction

THE UNITED STATES OF AMERICA was once recognized as the pinnacle of greatness. Our nation was once held in high esteem because of its leadership, which was built on Christian principles that were embedded in the very core of our foundation. America adopted as her motto, "In God We Trust", but has relinquished on the privilege of trusting God for His guidance and protection. Both ethical and moral standards have been etched as a distant memory in the minds of our leaders and now in many cases are a thing of the past. Homosexuality is on the rise. Divorce rates are soaring. Fornication, adultery, murder, crime and violence are rampant. Because of these issues and many others that we are facing today, it is clear that our nation has lost her focus.

So how did America get to the present situation? Surely, this did not happen overnight? I believe that several events have led to this point. One of the underlying problems lies in the fact that America has drifted away from God, and one clear indication of this is the very fact that prayer has been prohibited from our public school systems. The Ten Commandments have been mandated to be taken off the walls of schools and our court houses. Through advertising and media, society has conveyed the message that illicit sex is acceptable. With pornography on the rise, it appears that we are living in a modern day Sodom and Gomorrah.

Secondly, America became obsessed with the need to acquire more and more. America now operates under the law of greed and has adopted an "all about me" mentality. Everything is all about me and everything that I have is all for me. Give me any and everything as long as it brings me pleasure. She has taken God and his blessings for granted far too long and has traded the truth of God for deception, and embraced evil and called it good.

Is there hope for America? Yes, absolutely there is hope for America. But America must first reach a turning point and repent of her sins and seek God's face in spirit and truth. Jesus said in *II Chronicles 7:14 If my people who are called by my name, would humble themselves and pray, and seek my face and turn from their wicked ways, then I will hear from heaven and forgive their sin and heal their land.* If only America would humble herself before God, pray, and seek His face, and turn from her wicked ways, then, and only then can she be healed.

Not only has America as a nation lost her way, but many of us in our own personal lives have digressed from God's plan and alluded to following our own course of action. We have symbolically and metaphorically replaced God and his word with our own ideas, values and opinions. But just as there is hope for America, there is hope for those who have drift off course from God. Hence the focal point of the book is to offer hope and guidance to those individuals who have turned away from God and are seeking to be restored back to God and rebuild their relationship with Him.

DRIFTING OFF COURSE

Chapter 1

Therefore we ought to give the more earnest heed to the things which we have heard, lest at any time we should let them slip.
Hebrews 2:1

THERE ARE TIMES IN OUR lives that we may not feel as close to God. We may feel as though that God has distant himself from us. But rest assured it is not God who has moved. God has promised us that he will never leave us nor forsake us (Hebrew 13:5). So God is always there. During those times that we feel that God is not around, we should take spiritual inventory of our lives to see at what point we have become disengaged from God. If we look closely, we will find that oftentimes, this feeling of disassociation from God lays in the fact that we have misaligned our priorities. We have gotten caught up with the things that we think are so important that we have forgotten about what really is important, and that is to glorify God, seek to be in his presence and to get refreshed daily with His Holy Spirit.

Many times we are bombarded with the responsibility of taking care of our daily affairs that we somehow manage to ostracize God out our lives. It can easily start off by missing our daily prayer time or our intimate fellowship time with God.

Slowly, we begin to get lazy and passive about the things of the Lord such as reading the Word of God and attending worship services at our church. When we neglect these important things, we put ourselves in a position where it is easy to digress on the wrong course and drift away from God.

This does not happen overnight, but it is a slow gradual process. It can be so subtle that is possible to drift and not even know it. Imagine being in a boat in a river. You are relaxed and content, coasting along, enjoying the water. You are not really paying attention to the direction that you are going, and then suddenly you realize that you have drifted in the wrong direction. It is much the same way in the life of a Christian. We too can easily coast along life's path, enjoying everything that it has to offer only to find that we have drifted on the wrong path.

It is easy to drift away if you are not paying careful attention to the direction that you are going. When we allow our priorities to get in the wrong order, we are subject to stray away from the things that we know that are right to do. It can happen to any of us. Read the life story of Gayle, a devoted Christian who drifted off course and the effects that it had on her life.

In the beginning of her Christian journey, Gayle was on fire for God. She was excited about serving God, pleasing him and getting to know him better. She faithfully attended her church services and volunteered for every committee at her church that she could. She had such zeal to please God that she made a vow that she would always remain committed to him and would faithfully serve him until the day that she died. Her love for God was so intense and deeply rooted that she could never imagine turning away from him. But unfortunately just as so many other Christians have done, Gayle started to drift off course. She got her priorities in the wrong order, lost her focus and spiritually drifted from her first love. But how did this happen? What happened along the way that caused her to deviant off the path and drift from the love and protection of God to living a life of doom and gloom? What caused her to stray away from living a life of pleasing God to a life that focuses on only satisfying her needs and desires? How did she get to this point of backsliding?

It all began with the small decisions that she made in her everyday life that gradually led her away from God. Making more money, which required her to work more hours, became more important than spending time with God. Day by day she started spending less and less time reading her bible, and even less time praying. She eventually stopped attending Sunday morning worship services and midweek bible study. Gayle was no longer in fellowship with God and now because she did not seek Him for his guidance, she was in a position where she made decisions that did not line up with the Word of God. She no longer relied on God's word as her final authority, and as a result sin began to creep in. The things that she could never imagine herself getting involved in, were now a part of her everyday life. The more time that Gayle spent away from church and less time reading her bible, the further she drifted. The further that she drifted the more the sin became an active part of her life. Deep down in her heart, Gayle knew the right things to do, but she reached a point in her life where she no longer had the desire to do what was right. Her whole attitude had changed about sinning against God. In the beginning, she felt bad about sinning against Him, but as time went on she begin to justify what she was doing and she developed a nonchalant attitude about the sins that she had committed.

Like Gayle, we all start off with good intentions of faithfully serving God, but for some reason, some of us drift off course and sometimes regress back to a life of sin. The book of Hebrews gives several warnings about drifting. The first warning is recorded in Hebrews 2:1-3 reads *"Therefore we ought to give the more earnest heed to the things which we have heard, lest at any time we should let them slip. For if the word spoken by angels was stedfast, and every transgression and disobedience received a just recompense of reward. How shall we escape if we neglect so great salvation; which at the first began to be spoken by the Lord, and was confirmed unto us by them that heard him"*. This passage of scripture addresses the danger of being careless or thoughtless and not paying attention to the message of Jesus Christ. As Christians, we can hear the word again and again and not perceive it. We can become so accustomed to the word that we fail to truly hear it. It is one thing to listen and yet another thing to hear. We can listen to the Word of God as it is preached with our natural ears, but it is not until we hear it with our spiritual ears that we will see the results. The attitude of our heart shows what we hear. When we listen with our spiritual ears, then the Word of God will penetrate our hearts.

In Mark 4th chapter the parable of the sower speaks about four different kinds of listeners and their responses as it relates to the Word of God. The first was an *unresponsive listener.* The unresponsive listener hears the word, but before he can respond to the word the devil comes and takes it away from him. The *impulsive* listener hears the word, receives it with joy, but when trouble or persecution comes because of the word, they quickly fall away. The *preoccupied* listener hears the word, but does not pay full attention to it. His heart is deceived by the worries of this life, the deceitfulness of riches, and the desires for other things rather than the things of God. They are fruitless and choked by death. The good listener hears the word and gives it his fullest attention. He obeys the word and brings forth fruit. The question that we must each ask ourselves is, what kind of listener am I? We must purpose in our hearts and minds to be good listeners, and pay careful attention to the word of God because careless listening leads to drifting away from Christ.

How does the process of drifting begin? The process of drifting begins with *spiritual neglect.* According to Webster's dictionary, the word neglect means "to ignore or disregard; to fail to care for or attend to sufficiently or properly; to fail to carry out through carelessness or by intention; leave undone."

Most of us, if not all of us, would frown on a parent who neglects his or her child, because as parents it is our responsibility to take care of our children. If we don't feed them, provide clothes for them or most importantly, if we don't embrace them and show them love then we are neglecting our children. In a marital relationship, if the husband never expresses love for his wife, if he fails complement her, provide for her financially, then he is not fulfilling his role as a husband and he is neglecting his wife. The wife can neglect her husband needs as well. That is the same way it is with God. When we don't spend time with God, when we don't worship him, and when we don't read his word, we are neglecting him.

Satan knows that as believers that we would never openly rebellion against God so he executes ploys through our day to day affairs that will cause us to neglect God. Through his deceptive tactics, he will convince us to drop one church service, or one prayer meeting, or our intimate fellowship time with God. Satan will do anything that he can to sabotage our quality time with God. Think about this for a moment. Have you ever experienced a time that as soon as you started reading your bible, you began to get really sleepy? The time before you started to read you were fine but now you can barely keep your eyes open. You keep trying to read, but your head is nodding and your eyelids are about sealed shut. Why do you think that happens? Simply because Satan doesn't want you to read God's word. He knows that the more of God's word that you read, the stronger you will become. The stronger you become, the more power you will have to fight against him and win.

My friend that is only one of the many tactics that Satan can and will use. Satan wants us to drift one thought at a time, one small choice at a time, and often one damaging doubt at a time because he knows that the further we drift from God, the more danger we are in.

Although you may have once been on fire and excited about the truths of God, they will slip away from you if you don't pay attention to them. We should heed to the warning and keep spiritual truths before us, by reading and listening to the word of God, so that we don't drift back into unbelief. We can't afford to get too busy with other things and fail to pay proper attention to the things of God. We have too much at stake to neglect our salvation. Our salvation is too important to be ignored. Think about this for a moment: Have you ever driven in a neighborhood and saw how atrocious some of the houses and yards looked? The grass is overgrown and withering, the bushes needed trimming, tall weeds had sprouted up everywhere, the houses were rundown, and were in dire need of a paint job. It is a scene that depicts death. Why do you think that this neighborhood was in such condition? It is simply because the property had been neglected. No one has taken the time to do the necessary work that is required to keep the property up. It is much the same way with our spiritual lives. If we don't do what is needed so that we can remain committed to being a Christian, our lives will look just as atrocious. We will become rundown and washed out Christians. If we avoid reading our bible daily, engaging in prayer and spending quiet intimate time with God we become easy targets for Satan to cause us to neglect our faith. But it is when we implement these strategies that we are able to refrain from spiritually neglecting God.

Consequences of Drifting

If we allow ourselves to stray away from God there are consequences that we must face. It is a serious matter to God when we turn away from him. Ezekiel 33: 18 says *"When the righteous turneth from his righteousness, and committeth iniquity, he shall die"*. Jeremiah 17:5 says *"Thus saith the Lord; Cursed be the man that trusteth in man and maketh flesh his arm, and whose heart departeth from the Lord"*. We find the details of the curse in verse 6: *"For he shall be like the heathen in the desert, and shall not see when good cometh; but shall inhabit the parched places in the wilderness, in a salt land and not inhabited.*

When a person continues to drift from God, he will eventually experience what is known as spiritual dullness. This puts him in a position where his conscience becomes numb which ultimately leads to spiritual blindness and destruction. We become spiritually blind to the plots and schemes that Satan has devised to influence us to drift away from God. The problem of spiritual dullness prevents us from grasping the deeper truths of the Christian faith. Hebrews 5:11 addresses his readers about being dull or sluggish of hearing. In this passage of scripture, these believers should have been teachers of God's word, but instead they needed someone to teach them again. They had been believers long enough that they should be enjoying the meat of God's word, but yet they were still on the bottle. They had not grasped the foundational truths and as a result they were ineffective.

A person experiencing spiritual dullness can be described as slothful. Instead of progressing in the Christian life, the believer will become spiritually sluggish and mentally lazy as a result of drifting away from God. They have become dull of hearing. God is no longer the main focus in his life. The believer slips back into his old ways because he does not follow God's guidance and direction. He has become spiritually blind because he has removed himself from the Lord's presence and has stepped out of God's will for his life.

Another consequence of drifting away from God is being outside of His will. God has a plan for all of our lives. Jeremiah 29:11 says *"For I know the thoughts that I think toward you, saith the Lord, thoughts of peace, and not of evil, to give you an expected end"*. When we deviate from God's plan for our lives, we abort our destiny and our purpose. Drifting from God, puts us out of the boundaries of God's protection.

When we are out of Gods' will we are subject to become entangled with the sin of unbelief, which is another consequence that we face when we drift away from God. In Hebrews chapter 3 verse 12, says *"Take heed, brethren lest there be in any of you an evil heart of unbelief"*. Paul gave this warning to professing believers about the dangers of having an unbelieving heart and departing from God. This is the second warning that is given to us about departing away from God. This departing is the source of our word apostasy, which is the deliberate departure from God's full revelation. These Hebrew men were being tempted by an evil heart of unbelief to return to Judaism. This would mean that they would reject the full revelation of what they had received in Christianity and returned to the incomplete revelation of Judaism. They were instructed to exhort one another daily with the truths that will strengthen their faith in Christ.

Apostasy

Apostasy is the deliberate and permanent rejection of Christianity after a previous profession of faith in it. 1 Timothy 4:1 *says "Now the spirit speaketh expressly, that in latter times some shall depart from the faith, giving heed to seducing spirits, and doctrines of the devils"*. To depart means to apostatize. There are two main types of apostasy; a falling away from key and true doctrines of the Bible into heretical teachings that proclaim to be "the real" Christian doctrine; and a complete renunciation of the Christian faith, which results in a full abandonment of Christ. The characteristic of apostasy are a refusal to hear God, hardness of the heart, unbelief, open rebellion against God to provoke and tempt him, habitual sinning, careless living, and flagrant violation of God's laws, departure from God, all faith in

Christ and His redemptive work rejected. This kind of falling away is one that leads to eternal damnation.

It is dangerous for Christians to fully apostatize from Christ. According to Hebrews 10:26, *"For if we sin willfully after that we have received the knowledge of the truth, there remaineth no more sacrifice for sins"*, a person will not be able to ever find forgiveness. The blood of Jesus will not be able to cleanse them if they seek repentance. They will not have the faith to ask for forgiveness because their hearts will be hardened against God. They have denied the faith that is necessary to receive forgiveness. According to Hebrews 6:4-6, once a person has seen the light, and has had a taste of heaven and experienced the work of the Holy Ghost and the power of God's word, if they fall away, it is impossible to be brought back to repentance. It is just as if they are crucifying Jesus all over again and subjecting Him to public disgrace.

Discussion Questions

1. What are some ways that we can drift away from God?

_____

_____

_____

_____

_____

_____

_____

_____

_____

_____

_____

_____

_____

_____

_____

_____

_____

_____

_____

_____

_____

_____

2. In your own personal life, what areas have you drifted away from God?

_____

_____

_____

_____

_____

_____

_____

_____

_____

_____

_____

_____

_____

_____

_____

_____

_____

_____

_____

_____

3. What are scripture references that give us warnings about drifting away from God?

_____

_____

_____

_____

_____

_____

_____

_____

_____

_____

_____

_____

_____

_____

_____

_____

_____

_____

_____

_____

_____

_____

_____

4. What are some of the consequences of drifting away from God?

_____

_____

_____

_____

_____

_____

_____

_____

_____

_____

_____

_____

_____

_____

_____

_____

_____

_____

_____

_____

_____

_____

_____

NO EXEMPTION

Chapter 2

For all have sinned and fallen short of the glory of God.
Romans 3:23

N O CHRISTIAN IS EXEMPT FROM backsliding. It can happen to any of us. Even the most devoted believer can be subject to drifting away from God if we fall prey to one of Satan's tactics. I am not saying that everyone will turn their back on God. But I am saying that there is a possibility for all believers to stray away from God if we are not careful because we are still sinful imperfect Christians. As long as we are in our sinful bodies and in this fallen world, there is always a possibility for us to stray away from Christ. That is why we need to heed to the warning found in Hebrews 2:1. **"We must pay more careful attention, therefore, to what we have heard, so that we do not drift away"**.

Individuals can drift from God, but churches as a whole can drift as well. The bible gives several examples of churches that were once strong and dedicated to follow the principles of God, but ended up drifting. In Revelation chapter 2, we learn about how the church of Ephesus grieved Christ by drifting away from their first love. God knew all about their record. He knew about their works, labor and patience. He was aware of their intolerance of those who were evil and their ability to test those who claimed to be apostles, but found them to be liars. The church of Ephesus was commended because of its soundness of faith and it perseverance through persecution.

But God charged them because they had left their first love or their devotion to God. In verse 5, God gave the solution to the condition that they were in. The first thing that they needed to do was to remember their former devotion to Christ. Secondly, they needed to repent of the present lack of their love and devotion and finally, they needed to return or do the things that were characteristic of the devotion of the church of its earliest years.

The church of Pergamos was faithful to God in the respect that they remained true to his name. They didn't renounce their faith even under the worst circumstances when their faith was put to the test. But in some respect, they were not faithful because they had those who taught the doctrine of Balaam to be in their midst. The doctrine of Balaam was a compromise of Christianity with paganism, resulting in idolatry and immorality. Balaam had once succeeded in leading many Israelites into sins.

In the church at Thyatira, a self proclaimed prophetess who God called Jezebel was allowed to teach and to seduce men of God to commit fornication and to eat things sacrificed for idols. God gave her an opportunity to repent. She refused to repent therefore she would he judged along with all her followers.

Likewise, the Laodicea church drifted into lukewarmness, and the church at Sardis drifted into spiritual death. (Revelation chapter 3). Paul warns the believers in Galatia that they had drifted from the victory of Christ's cross and had turned back to works of their flesh.

The bible also gives us examples of true saints of God, people who loved the Lord and were dedicated to following him, but yet fell into the trap of sin and as a result were in a backslidden position at one point in their lives.

Noah planted his vineyard, he drank some of the wine and became drunk and lay uncovered in his tent. (Genesis chapter 9)

Lot sought the fellowship of the wicked Sodomites, lost all his influence, got drunk and ruined his own daughters.(Genesis ch.19)

Abraham deceived Pharaoh into thinking that his wife Sarah was his sister. (Genesis chapter 12)

Moses lost his temper when God commanded him to speak to the rock that Israel might be watered from it a second time. He disobeyed

God and instead of speaking to the rock, he beat it. Because of this he lost his chance to enter the Promised Land. (Numbers 20th chapter)

Samson kept company with harlots until God left him powerless, a slave of the Philistines with his eyes burned out. (Judges 16th chapter)

Peter denied Christ and cursed and swore (Matthew 26th).

Judas Iscariot betrayed Jesus for thirty pieces of silver (Matthew 26:14-16).

The men of Ephraim, though armed with bows, turned back on the day of battle: they did not keep God's covenant and refused to live by His law. Psalms 78:9-11

Asa was a king of Judah. According to II Chronicles 14:2 records that *"Asa did what was good and right in the eyes of the Lord His God."* He was described as having a heart that was *"fully committed to the Lord all his life."* (II Ch.15:17) Although Asa started off good, he soon fell away. Although the Lord had saved his kingdom before, when his enemies came up against Judah, Asa did not turn to the Lord for help this time. Instead, he turned to a neighboring king and offered him silver and gold out of the treasuries from the Lord's temple. The Lord sent a messenger to tell Asa that because he had not turned to God for help, his enemies would escape his hand and war would continue throughout his reign.

By these examples in the Bible, we see that no one immune from falling into sin. These examples should humble us and teach us that even the mightiest of God's saints sometimes even backslide and fall into the trap of sin. Regardless of how close we walk with God, no matter how long we have served Him, we all remain susceptible to the temptations of sin and drifting away from Christ.

Read this touching story about a famous Christian hip-hop gospel artist who shared his testimony about how he drifted away from God. He started by saying that he was a father, husband, brother and a man of God. He grew up living in a home with both his father and his mother. His mother was firm, but loving and fun. He and his family spent a great deal of time in church. When he got older, he went to college. Now living on his own, he thought that he had the freedom to do whatever he wanted to do. He thought he was grown and didn't have to listen to anyone. He started to stray away from church. He says that he didn't want any part of church because of the music (hip-hop RB) that he was interested in did not belong in the church. He devised a plan and set a goal to sell a lot of records and then he would give the money to the church. He would then settle down and start doing gospel records. He eventually opened a studio on his college campus. In the beginning he had a rule that he would not make any music that his mom could not listen to but He began to make records for drug dealers. The lyrics of the song had words that he didn't approve of, but because of the money that he was being paid he let it slide. The more money that he made, the more willing he was to compromise. He felt that he had to compromise because he was chasing his dreams and the people that he was making records for had all the right connections. He admits that he made a lot of bad decisions. He had become a person that he was not proud of.

There were a lot of situations that he could have lost his life, but God spared his life. One incident that he recalled that changed his life happened in his studio. A guy had come into his studio armed with a fully loaded weapon looking for a particular person. It turned out that it was not the person that he was looking for. It was a case of mistaken identity.

His studio was broken into and equipment was stolen. He called his all of his guys to the studio. They came fully armed with their weapons. He wanted to get revenge but he couldn't. He started to cry and told his guys to go home. He said he started to wonder how did he get this far, here he was a child of God, with a hit out on a man's life. He knew then that he had gone too far. His wife took him to church and he heard the preacher, preach about the righteous of God. He heard something in the word that changed his life.

As Christian, we don't have to fall and drift away from God, if we heed to the warnings given to us throughout the word of God. It was the word of God that changed this hip hop gospel artist's life, and the word of God can change your life too.

Remember even the strongest Christian can fall. Don't rely on the fact that you have been in church a long time. That fact alone does not exempt you from drifting away. You must stay rooted and grounded in the Word of God and heed to the warnings that God gives to us.

Discussion Questions

1. Give some Biblical examples of a person falling back into sin.

_____

_____

_____

_____

_____

_____

_____

_____

_____

_____

_____

_____

_____

_____

_____

_____

_____

_____

_____

_____

_____

_____

_____

2. In what ways can you identify with the testimony that was shared in this chapter?

_____

_____

_____

_____

_____

_____

_____

_____

_____

_____

_____

_____

_____

_____

_____

_____

_____

_____

_____

_____

_____

_____

3. What are some biblical examples of churches drifting from God?

_____

_____

_____

_____

_____

_____

_____

_____

_____

_____

_____

_____

_____

_____

_____

_____

_____

_____

_____

_____

_____

_____

_____

ARE YOU COMMITTING SPIRITUAL ADULTERY?

Chapter 3

Ye adulters and adulteress, know ye not that the friendship
of the world is enmity with God? Whosoever therefore will
be a friend of the world is the enemy of God. James 4:4

THE MARITAL RELATIONSHIP IS ONE of the most important
relationship besides your relationship with Jesus Christ. It is a
sacred relationship between a man and a woman who have pledged
their faithfulness to each other until death. According to scripture
this bond between husband and wife supercedes the relationship the
parent and the child. Genesis 2:24 says *'Therefore shall a man leave
his father and mother and shall cleave unto his wife".* The marriage
relationship is so significant that God used it as an illustration for his
special love for his people.

Marriage is an institution created by God and is a continuation of
His work of creation. It is honorable in his eyesight. Hebrews 13;4 says
*"Marriage is honorable in all, and the bed undefiled: but whoremongers
and adulterers God will judge".* The marriage relationship should be
honored by all and the bed must be kept pure. When things such
as adultery that occur outside the boundaries of the confinement of
marriage, that the relationship becomes tainted. We are all familiar
with the word adultery in the natural. We have either committed
adultery ourselves or we know of someone who has. Webster defines it

as two people engaging in sexual intercourse with a person other than their spouse. Adultery is the ultimate act of betrayal and often times shatter lives and destroys marriages. The media portrays a false illusion that adultery can be used as a tool to put spice back in your life, but on the contrary it usually does the opposite.

Think for a moment how you would feel after all the love that you have shown your spouse, all the time you have invested in your relationship, all the sacrifices you have made, you discover that your spouse has not been faithful. What kinds of emotions do you think you would experience? My guess would be that you would probably feel hurt, disappointed, embarrassed, outraged, and definitely betrayed. Now think for a moment how God feels when we put other people before him and when we neglect him. Think how much pain we put him through when we are not faithful. God feels outrage and jealous when we betray him by giving our love, and devotion to someone or something else. God feels the same emotions that we do, just on a deeper level.

We are in a covenant relationship with God. When we sin against Him we break that covenant. Furthermore, when we are not faithful to him, we are committing spiritual adultery. The Israelites were guilty of committing spiritual adultery. Israel had been unfaithful to God by following other gods and breaking God's commandments thereby breaking the terms of the covenant.

Marriage was symbolic of the covenant relationship between God and Israel. The book of Hosea gives an account of how the Israelites rebelled against God and as a result broke their covenant with him. The charges that God brought against Israel was that there was no faithfulness, kindness or knowledge of Him. There was swearing, deception, murder, stealing and sexual vice. The prophets and priests were corrupt. The priests were no longer teaching the knowledge of God. The religious leaders were making a profit from the sins of the people. There was harlotry and drunkeness and the people had become idol worshippers.

As a part of his redemption plan, God used Hosea to confront Israel with their sin of unfaithfulness. The story begins by God telling Hosea *"to go take to yourself a wife of whoredoms and have children of whoredoms, for the land committed great whoredoms, departing from the Lord"*. (Hosea 1:2)

Can you imagine entering into a covenant relationship with a person knowing first hand that the person is not going to be faithful? This is an assignment that I am sure that none of us would want, but God had a reason behind why he told Hosea to do what he did. That reason was to redeem his people.

Hosea did exactly what God told him to do. He married a prostitute by the name of Gomer. Through this union, three children were conceived. Each child was given a name which was symbolic of Israel's relationship to God. The first child was named Jezreel which means God sows. This was an indication of what would happen to Israel because of her disobedience.

The second child was given the name, Lo-ruhamah, which means no compassion. God would no longer have compassion on Israel, but would bring judgement on them. The third child was named Lo-ammi. This name meant "not my people". This indicated that Israel was not God's people and He was not their God. God would no longer protect Israel and now Israel was in the position of facing the consequences for their actions. He would not have compassion because they had given credit to foreign gods and nations for their provision of water, wool, flax, oil and drink. If God had continued to protect Israel from the consequences of their sins, they would have never understood the devastation of the choices that they had made and perhaps never would have turned back to him.

We learn in chapter 2 how God confronts Israel's spiritual adultery and the consequences that they would face if they did not repent for their sins. God told Hosea to plead with his mother because he declared that He was not longer Israel's husband and she was not his wife. The prophet uses his personal domestic tragedy as a means of addressing not only his own children and their mother, but also the believing remnant who in turn are to plead with their mother (Israel) to return back to God. Israel broke the marriage covenant and this was a dangerous position to be in. That is why God was pleading with Israel to change her adulterous ways. But if she didn't respond to the call of repentance, God made it clear the consequences that she would have to face. According to Chapter 2 verse 3, God was going to strip her naked, and expose her as the day she was born. He would make her as a wilderness, and set her like a dry land, and slay her with thirst. He would have no compassion on her children because they were the product of prostitution.

It is essential that as believers we take the time to examine our lives to see if have lost our spiritual awareness and are in danger of committing spiritual adultery. Make a vow to remain committed to God. Sometimes when a person thinks that the grass is greener on the other side they will be tempted to check it out for themselves. That is what Satan does. He makes what he has to offer look appealing and inviting. Don't allow Satan to entice you to cheat on God. God does not want any "part time lovers". He wants you to be fully committed to Him.

Common Signs Of A Spiritual Cheater

Below are some common signs that a person is cheating on God.

1. ***Poor church attendance***—A person who is cheating or has already cheated usually has poor church attendance. In the beginning, they may attend a few church services occasionally, but then they will start to drop one service at a time, until eventually they are no longer attending church on a regular basis. They come to church when they feel like it. They allow other activities to take the place of faithfully attending church.

2. ***Decreased fellowship with Jesus*-,** A person who is cheating does not make time to fellowship with Jesus. He or she allows distractions to hinder him or her from spending intimate time with Jesus. Everything else takes top priority over spending quiet and quality time with Jesus.

3. ***Living an undisciplined Life***—A spiritual cheater's life is undisciplined and out of order. He or she does not make the effort to exercise discipline in his or her life, but instead goes against the boundaries established in their relationship with God. It is just like in a marriage relationship between a man and a woman, there are boundaries that have been established in their relationship. They have made a vow to be faithful to each other, forsaking all others. If there were no guidelines set, then it would be perfectly all right to be married and have a girlfriend or boyfriend on the side. But it

is not okay because you have committed yourself to loving to that one special person that you made a sacred vow too. Therefore you should invest all of your time and energy in loving that person. So it is with our spiritual marriage to God. When we enter into a covenant relationship with him, we pledged to be faithful to him, forsaking all other gods. You see, just as there are boundaries in our relationship with our spouse, there are boundaries in our relationship with God. We can not be in relationship with God and flirting with other gods that we have created.

4. **Serving other gods**—When a person is spiritually cheating on God, they have other gods at the center of their hearts. Having anything other than God at the center of our hearts becomes what is known as an idol. An idol is person, or addiction or pleasure, or material things such as our house, cars, money that cause us to drift away from God. Those things become more important and mean more to the cheater more than God does. In Matthew 6: 24, it says *"No man can serve two masters: for either he will hate the one, and love the other; or else he will hold to the one, and despise the other. Ye cannot serve God and mammon"*. True loyalty can not be divided between God and your idols.

5. **No longer have a desire to study God's word.**
   If you are not studying and reading your bible then you are in danger of straying away from God. The less you study the Word of God, the more and the further you will drift. The Word of God is compromised of 66 intimate love letters written to us from God. 2 Timothy 3: 16 gives us the reason that God gave us the written word of God. *"All scripture is given by inspiration of God, and is profitable for doctrine, for reproof, for correction, for instruction in righteousness"*. The Bible is our guide in how we are to conduct ourselves and live a holy life. It helps us to mature spiritually. 1 Peter 2:1, Paul says that we should desire the sincere milk of the word, that ye may grow thereby. When you don't have a desire to study God's word, then you do not grow up spiritually. When you do not grow up spiritually, then your spiritual progress is hindered. When you are not making progress, you become stagnated. If you have lost your desire to study God's word, you are on the path to becoming a spiritual cheater!

6. ***No longer have a desire to fellowship with other Christians.*** A spiritual cheater does not have a desire to fellowship with other believers. This goes beyond the parameters of fellowship at church. When a person is drifting from God, often times the last person that he might want to see is a believer. He does not want to have any association with a person who will confront him or make him think twice about the lifestyle he is living.

7. ***Lack the desire to share the Gospel.*** When you as a Christian no longer have the desire to share the message of Jesus Christ you are in danger of cheating. Do you remember the first time you feel in love? That person was always on your mind. You thought about him or her all the time and about talked about him or her to anybody who would listen. That's how special that person was to you. That is how it should be with Jesus. He should be on our minds and we should think about him everyday. He should be so special to us that we want to share him with anybody who will listen.

8. ***Enticed by the things of the world***—If you find more pleasure in worldly activities than Godly activities, then you are in danger of being a spiritual cheater. Satan has a way to make the things of the world and his way of doing things seem more appealing to the eye. When we become intrigued with the things of the world, we lose focus. It is hazardous to our spiritual health when we get entangled with the cares of this world. That is why the word of God tells us in Colossians 3:2 to *"set our affections on things above, not on things on the earth"*.

There may be other signs that would indicate that you are on the course of drifting from God or have already drifted.

If you have not been faithful to God and if you have strayed then it is my prayer that you will ask for forgiveness and recommit to being faithful to God again. God is pleading with you to turn from your adulterous ways. If you are ready to recommit yourself and be a faithful partner in your marriage to Jesus, then feel free to pray this prayer: Father I acknowledge that I have strayed away from you. I have not been faithful and because of my unfaithfulness I have broken the covenant between us. I ask for your forgiveness. I want to turn back to you and recommit my life to you. Help me to be a faithful partner.

Discussion Questions

1. Can you identify with any of the signs of being a spiritual cheater in your life?

_____

_____

_____

_____

_____

_____

_____

_____

_____

_____

_____

_____

_____

_____

_____

_____

_____

_____

_____

_____

_____

2. What can you do to become faithful to God again?

_____

_____

_____

_____

_____

_____

_____

_____

_____

_____

_____

_____

_____

_____

_____

_____

_____

_____

_____

_____

_____

_____

_____

_____

_____

WHY CHRISTIANS GO AWOL?

Chapter 4

Having a form of godliness, but denying the power thereof:
from such turn away. 2Timothy 3:5

I F WE ARE IN TUNE with how much God loves us, and we realize the danger of drifting, then why do we allow ourselves to drift? Why are so many Christians living defeated, broken lives? Why have so many born-again believers fallen prey to the temptations of this world when God has promised a way of escape? Why have so many Christians gone AWOL(Absent Without Leave)? This term generally applies to the military and refers to when the personnel are absent from their post without a valid pass or leave. But this term can certainly be viewed from a spiritual standpoint as well, because so many Christians have abandoned their post in the army of the Lord. But why have they forsaken the Lord? The answer is quite simple: It is because of sin. Sin is the root cause of why people drift away from God. Sin can be defined as *any deviation from God's perfect standard of holiness.* This can be the result of our thoughts, our behavior or in what we say. As a result of sin, we reject God and instead put ourselves in His place. This means that sin is not only the fact of our separation from God, but also involves our willful disobedience. When we willfully disobey God, we fall into the entrapment of sin, which will take us down a path we never intended to go.

Let's examine the life of King David, the greatest king of Israel. King David, the son of Jesse, and one of the most prominent Bible characters, was a man after God's own heart. He was used by God to write a great portion of the book of Psalm. He was a shepherd boy who defeated the giant Goliath. Even with all of these victories and so many more, David still drifted away from God at one point in his life. In the book of 2 Samuel chapter 11 we learn about David's love affair with Bathsheba. It was the time of year that kings were to be in battle, but instead of going himself, David sent Joah and his servants and all of Israel. He stayed in Jerusalem. This proved to be the starting point of David's problems. Had he been where he was suppose to be, perhaps he would not have been tempted to do what he did. The Bible says that David got out of his bed and went on the roof of his house and watched a woman by the name of Bathsheba take a bath. Enticed by her beauty, David inquired about her and eventually had intimate relations with her. During the moment of passion, Bathsheba conceived. Stricken with terror, David strategized a plan to cover up his sin and shift the responsibility to someone else. Uriah, Bathsheba husband was a faithful warrior who was out on the battlefield. David called him from the battle and told him to go down to his house assuming that he would have sex with Bathsheba. In so doing, Uriah would think that the baby was his. But because of Uriah' s loyalty and honor for his fellow commorades, David's plan did not work. Uriah would not go and enjoy the pleasures of home while the others were still in battle. David's attempt to get Uriah drunk, was to no avail. He still would not go to his house. Out of pure desperation, David resorted to the unthinkable. He told Joab, the leader of the kings army to put Uriah in a place where he would be killed. King David's affair with Bathsheba is the perfect example of how falling into the trap of sin can cause you to drift from God.

Sin is the underlying cause of drifting from God, and Satan and his demons are the force behind a Christian turning from his faith. As believers, we cannot afford to underestimate Satan's power to cause us to go AWOL. Satan strategically plans how he can destroy our relationship with God. He uses your mind as his target and his lies as his weapon. John 8:44 says *"Ye are of your father the devil, and the lusts of your father ye will do. He was a murderer from the beginning and abode not in the truth, because there is no truth in him. When he speaketh a lie, he speaketh of his own: for he is a liar, and the father of it."* If Satan can get you to believe his lies, then he can begin to work in your life to lead you into sin. Satan is subtle and he is such a deceiver. He knows how to play on your every weakness, he knows how to capitalize on your all fears. He knows every scripture in the Bible and he knows how to use them to his advantage to entrap you. Ephesians 4:27 says "Neither give place the devil". That means don't give Satan an opportunity or space to cause you to sin. All he really needs is a little space in your mind then he can begin the process of deceiving you. When you allow Satan to invade your life, he puts you in the position where he can work in your life that will ultimately lead you into sin.

As Christians, we must have an understanding of who Satan is and how he operates. The Bible gives us several descriptions of Satan's personality to help us to identify who he is. He is subtle, crafty and cunning. St. John 8:44 describes him as the father of lies. He is also known as the deceiver as recorded in Revelation 12:9: *"And the great dragon was cast out, that old serpent, called the Devil, and Satan, which deceiveth the whole world: he was cast out into the earth, and his angels were cast out with him".* He displayed his role as the great deceiver in the story of Adam and Eve. God gave both Adam and Eve clear instructions that they could eat from any tree in the garden except the tree of the knowledge of good and evil. If they did eat from the tree of the knowledge of good and evil or even touch the tree, they would die. Satan started the implementation of his evil plot to deceive Eve, by posing a question to her. With his cunning demeanor, he asked the question, "Did God really say that you could not eat from any tree in the garden?" Eve demonstrated her understanding of God's instructions in her response to Satan: "We may eat fruit from the tree in the garden, but God did say, you must not eat fruit from the tree that is in the middle of the garden, and you must not touch it, or you will die". Although Eve knew what God had said, she allowed Satan, to deceive her in eating the fruit from the tree of the knowledge of good and evil. Not only did Eve eat the fruit, but she also convinced Adam to eat from the tree as well. Because of Satan's deception and Adam and Eve's disobedience, God issued a punishment for each of them. To Satan he told him, that he would be cursed above all the livestock and all the wild animals. He would crawl on his belly and eat dust all the days of his life. There would be enmity between Satan and the woman and between his offspring and her offspring. Eve was cursed with having pains that would be greatly multiplied during childbirth. The ground was cursed as a result of Adam's sin and now he had to till the ground to get food for him and wife.

Before they had eaten off this forbidden tree, the Bible tells us that Adam and Eve were literally allowed to run naked in the garden. They had no shame in doing this. But after they had eaten from the tree, their eyes were opened and they knew their nakedness. They sowed fig leaves together to cover their nakedness. For the first time, Adam and Eve experienced the feeling of guilt and shame. This is precisely the underlying reason why God did not want them to eat from the tree of the knowledge of good and evil. Satan had convinced Eve to believe that God did want her to eat from the tree because she would be as knowledgeable as him, but in essense that was not the case at all, God was trying to protect them from the knowledge of evil. It was God's plan that they never be exposed to evil and engage in sin, because he knew once they did the end result would be death.

Not only did Adam and Eve mess things up for themselves, but for the rest of the human race. Every since the fall of mankind, Satan still tries to convince as many Christians as he can to disobey God and deviant off the path that God had predestined for them.

There are other causes that can be attributed to personal reasons why some Christians stop living a dedicated life for Christ. One reason is discouragement. Although Galatians 6:9 encourages us not *to grow weary in well doing, for in due season we shall reap, if we faint not,* Christians sometimes still get discouraged. A litany of problems can bring a sense of discouragement in the life of a believer. Even the simplest form of discouragement can lead a Christian to doubting his faith in God. It can put a Christian in a position of losing hope in the ability to maintain the momentum to be a good soldier in the Jesus' army and fight the good fight of faith until the end. 2 Timothy 2:3 says "Thou therefore endure hardness, as a good soldier of Jesus Christ". As soldiers, we will experience hardships. We will have trials and tribulations in our life. Trials are an inevitable part of reality in life. James 1:2 says, "My brethren, count it all joy when you fall into divers temptation". Notice this scripture did not say, if you fall, but when you fall into divers temptation, which means various trials. Trials are inescapable. Jesus said "These things I have spoken unto you, that in me ye might have peace. In this world, ye shall have tribulation: but be of good cheer, I have overcome the world". (John 16:33).

It is certain that we will all have trials and our faith will indeed be put to the test, but what makes the difference of whether we pass or fail our test is how we react when we experience hardship. Many Christians become discouraged and overwhelmed when they are put to the test. When they seek God to find the answer to the infamous question, "why me"? "Why am I going through what I am going through"? They become discouraged when God answers back "why not you"? We become even more discouraged when we pray that our trials will quickly end, but God has a another plan on his agenda, that will require us to endure the test a little while longer. God uses trials to test our faith. When we go through trials, our faith is tested to validate what we declare we believe. Instead of complaining about going through test or allowing ourselves to become discouraged because of our trials, we should focus our attention on seeking God to find out what he wants us to learn from the test. In every test that God allows to happen in our lives, there is a lesson that he wants us to learn. We can pass our test and defeat the demon called discouragement when we focus on the problem solver, rather than the problem itself.

Another reason that we sometimes drift is because we focus too much attention on the cares of the world. We are often bombarded with the constant pressures of daily cares and responsibilities. If we are not careful, we will allow the cares of the world distract us from the purpose for which we have been called. That is exactly what Satan wants. His purpose is to render us ineffective for the Kingdom. He seeks to strip us of our spiritual strength. His objective is to crowd our lives with his interests.

Jesus warned against this on several occasions *(Lu 21:34) And take heed to yourselves, lest at any time your hearts be overcharged with surfeiting, and drunkenness, and cares of this life, and so that day come upon you unawares.* We often let distractions get us easily off course and cause us to drift away from God.

Another reason we drift is the loss of our devotion to God. Devotion to God encompasses more than being an active church member or visiting the sick, but it equates to how faithful we are at keeping Him first in our lives. Like the church of Ephesus, some of us are guilty of losing our first love. **(Rev. *2:4*)** *Nevertheless I have somewhat against thee, because thou hast left thy first love.* We are not as devoted as we once were because we have allowed so many other people and things to take top priority in our life. God wants to be the driving force behind why you do what you do. He is more concerned about our devotion to Him, rather than all the activities that we do. We should operate out of love for God, rather than out of obligation.

Jesus warned us that in the last days because of sin in the world, many believers will become cold in their love for Christ (Matthew 24:12). My friend, if you have you grown cold in your heart toward your devotion to God, then now is the time to adjust your spiritual thermostat. There will be some who will grow cold in their love for Christ, but that does not have to include you. Jesus also said those who stand firm to the end will be saved. Make a decision today to stand firm in your devotion and love for God until the end so that you can be saved.

When we allow ourselves to get too busy and lose focus we are in danger of drifting from God. Believe it or not we can become too busy doing Godly things. We can get too involved in doing things "for" God that we miss doing things "with" God such as spending quality time with him. Please don't misunderstand me, it is important to do the things necessary to build God's kingdom. But I must reiterate the fact that we need to periodically have a spiritual checkup to monitor our motives. If we are working out of pure love and devotion for Christ, then great. But sometimes we get too busy and we forget the most important thing and that is to glorify God. One of Satan's tactics is too keep us busy so that we don't focus on getting closer to God. I was watching a David Jeremiah television broadcast and I heard him say something very interesting about Satan tactics to get the victory over Christians. In the story that he told, Satan had apparently called a worldwide convention with his angels. As Satan began his opening address, he said to his angels, "We can't keep Christians from going to church. We can't keep them from reading the Bible and knowing the truth. We can't even keep them from forming an intimate abiding experience in Christ. If they gain that connection with Jesus Christ, our power over them is broken. So let them go to their churches; let them have their conservative lifestyles, but steal their time so they can't gain that relationship with Jesus Christ. Keep them busy in the nonessential things of life". My friend that was Satan's mission then and it is still his mission today. He wants o keep us focused on things that seem important so that we will operate under his command. In fact, some have said that being "busy" means Being Under Satan's Yoke. Satan's mission is to steal, kill and destroy. He wants to steal your time, kill your devotion to God and destroy your relationship with Him.

It may be hard to fathom the idea of receiving God's blessings as one of the causes as to why some drift away from God. But it is quite possible for us to get too comfortable with God blessing us. That is what happened to the Israelites. With his prophetic eye, Moses looked into the future and saw how the Israelites would become too complacent with the blessings and how they would begin to drift away from God. So he gave them a warning *"Take heed to thyself, and keep thy soul diligently, lest thou forget the things which thine eyes have seen, and lest they depart from thy heart all the days of thy life"* *(verse 9)*. Moses gave them this warning at the very beginning. "Beware that thou forget not the Lord thy God, in not keeping his commandments, and his judgments, and his statutes . . . lest when thou hast eaten and art full, and hast built goodly houses, . . . and thy silver and thy gold is multiplied, and all that thou hast is multiplied; then thine heart be lifted up, and thou forget the Lord thy God, which brought thee forth out of the land of Egypt, from the house of bondage" (Deuteronomy 6:11-14).

Moses was letting the Israelites that know it won't be because of idolatry that they would drift away from God but rather because of the good life. Their spiritual senses will be dulled by ease, prosperity, blessings and fullness. They would be so wrapped up in good things that they would forget the Lord. God would quickly fade away from their mind and they would drift away from Him.

Although Moses warned them, the Israelites did not listen. They said within themselves, that they would never neglect God. But they did. Satan knew that he could not entice them to turn from God through sensuality and lust, but he used riches and blessings.

Unfortunately some Christians like the Israelites did not heed to Moses' warning. They have fallen into the same trap that the Israelites did and have gotten too comfortable with their blessings and have forgotten about God. They have barricaded in their minds that God is the only source of all their blessings, and without Him they would not be blessed. In some Christian's lives, it is sometimes, easier to reach out to the Lord in times of hardship and trials rather than times of blessings. When things are going good in their life, all the bills are paid, the children are not sick, they got a promotion on their job, the husband and wife are getting along well, then they don't feel the need to talk to God as much. But my friend that is how they get off course. God wants to bless us and takes pleasure in doing so. In fact it says in Psalm 35:27 "Let them shout for joy, and be glad, that favour my righteous cause: yea, let them say continually, Let the Lord be magnified, which hath pleasure in the prosperity of his servant". But he does not want us to allow His favor and blessings put us in danger of putting him on the backburner in our lives. I believe Moses was speaking to us as well when he said to Israel, "Beware lest thou forget the Lord, which brought thee forth!" (Deuteronomy 6:12).

Finally another reason that we drift away from God is simply because we want to do things our way and refuse to follow God's direction. We often times rebel against him and sometimes he has to resort to drastic measures to get us back on the right track. Jonah is the prime candidate to illustrate this point. Jonah was a prophet of God, and God had given him instructions to go to Nineveh. God told Jonah "Arise and go to Nineveh, that great city, and cry against it; for their wickedness is come up before me". But instead of going to Nineveh, Jonah went to Joppa. He bought a ticket on a cargo ship headed for Tarshish. This city was known for its mighty ships and precious metals. It was a city that represented prosperity, success and power. Jonah got on board the ship went down into the hold of the ship, wrapped himself in a blanket and fell asleep. God orchestrated a storm to get Jonah's attention. Without warning the winds became violent, the waves rose higher and the sails were ripped apart. Jonah slept through it all. Jonah was thrown overboard and swallowed by a fish. He stayed in the fish for three days. Realizing that he had made a mistake, he turned back to God.

It took three days and nights in the belly of a fish for Jonah to turn back to God and carry out the mission that God had for him, what will it take for you? How far will you let yourself drift away from God and his plan for your life before you turn back? How long will it take before you seek the Lord for forgiveness and be restored back into fellowship with Him? You can not escape from God. If you are living in disobedience, you can rest assure that God will do whatever it takes to get your attention, to get you back on the right track even if it means going through a great trial. Your trial could be a concerning your health, finances or your family. Your family and friends may try to protect you from the storm, but to no avail. God has a divine purpose for sending a storm in your life, and no one can hinder his plan. He will not allow you to walk away from him because he has too much of an investment in you and that is His only begotten Son, Jesus Christ. If you have dropped out of God's army it is time to get back on the battlefield and fight for the Lord. You must make the decision to follow Jesus and to live a fully committed life. Just as a soldier who has committed to bear arms for his country, can not quit in the midst of a battle, you must not become AWOL as warriors for Christ.

Discussion Questions

1. What does it mean when a Christian goes AWOL?

_____

_____

_____

_____

_____

_____

_____

_____

_____

_____

_____

_____

_____

_____

_____

_____

_____

_____

_____

_____

_____

_____

2. What are some reasons that Christians go AWOL?

_____

_____

_____

_____

_____

_____

_____

_____

_____

_____

_____

_____

_____

_____

_____

_____

_____

_____

_____

_____

_____

_____

WHAT HAPPENS WHEN WE BACKSLIDE?

Chapter 5

And Jesus said unto him, No man having put his hand to the plough, and looking back is fit for the kingdom of God.
Luke 9:62

I CAN RECALL A TIME that I have set a goal to lose weight. Grant it there had been many times before, but this time I was very adamant about losing weight. I went to a four week seminar to learn about the nutritious foods that were healthy for me to eat and the types of exercises that I needed to do in order to reach my goal. I was equipped with the information that I needed to embark on the journey of reaching my goal to lose weight. I changed my eating habits (cut out fried foods, ate more vegetables and fruits, increased water intake, eliminated sodas from diet) and I incorporated morning and afternoon walks in my schedule. It took some time getting adapted to living a healthier lifestyle, but I knew that the dividends would be worth the time and effort that I had invested. Things were going really good while I was taking the class during that four week period. I was sticking with the plan that I had created to help me reach my goal. A month passed by, I was so proud of myself because I was still on track and had actually lost four pounds. I was both excited about my progress and motivated to keep moving forward. I was making progress for a while, but slowly over time I started to regress back to some of my old habits. Instead of walking morning and evenings, I only walked in the mornings. I started back eating the late night snacks while watching television. I didn't monitor my sweets intake as much as I needed too. Habits like these were the reasons that I was in the position of needing to lose weight in the first place. I knew that this was not indicative of a healthy lifestyle, but yet these are the choices that I made. I backslide from the truth and from what I knew was the right thing to do. I regressed back to some of my old eating habits.

This is what happens in the life of some Christians. When a born again believer falls back into their sins and turns away from God, they are backsliding. Backsliding can happen to any Christian who does not resist temptation and allows sin to overtake their lives. This sin can be an open rebellion that is publicly known by others or it can be a private matter of a Christian allowing his heart to grow cold in their devotion to God.

Proverbs 14:14 says "The backslider in heart shall be filled with his own ways: and a good man shall be satisfied from himself". Backsliding is a heart condition. It is quite possible to have something going on in your heart even before the symptoms manifest. Most people identify the backslider as being the person who has fallen into sin and has turned away from God, but it is possible for a person to have backslidden in their heart even though they are in church every week.

When a Christian backslides, they put themselves in a position where they no longer seek the Lord's guidance, therefore they lack direction. They are no longer in fellowship with God and because of that they have an empty void left in their lives. This void can only be filled by Jesus Christ because we were created to have a relationship with him. But yet the backslider attempts to fill this void with other things that give him only a temporary satisfaction.

The condition of the backslider's heart changes from faithfully loving and serving God to a state of operating under the influence of Satan. Satan becomes their commanding officer and is the driving force behind everything that the backslider does. I am reminded of the story of Ananias and his wife Sapphira found in Acts chapter 5. Ananias and Sapphira sold a possession. They kept back part of the price and put a certain part at the apostle' s feet. Peter asked them, Why has Satan filled thine heart to lie to the Holy Ghost and to keep back part of the price of the land? The reason that they lied to the Holy Ghost was because they were operating under the influence of Satan.

One of the greatest attributes of being a good parent is to love and protect your children. Every good parent wants to protect their child from the dangers of the world, from the temptation to follow the wrong crowd and being enticed by Satan's schemes and ploys. Every good parent has a desire for their child to fulfill their purpose, maximize their full potential and walk in their destiny. Our heavenly Father shares the same desire, just at a deeper level. God does not want His children to get caught up in Satan's traps. He wants us to fulfill our purposes that he has predestined for us even before we were born. He has a desire for us to maximize our full potential and grow into the sons and daughters that he has called us to be. He wants to protect us from the danger of the world, but when we backslide, we are not under God's divine protection.

In Psalm 23:1, David made a personal declaration confessing that God is his shepherd. He says, "The Lord is my shepherd, I shall not want". A shepherd is one who takes care of sheep. Jesus says in John 10:11, "I am the good shepherd. The good shepherd lays down his life for the sheep". Our heavenly Father is our shepherd and we are his sheep. As his sheep we are completely depend on him for his guidance, provision and protection. When we allow our shepherd to guide us, we have his protection. He will guide us to the green pastures and quiet waters. When we are tempted to go our own way instead of the God's way then we put ourselves in danger.

I remember watching an episode on a particular animal channel. There were several big ferocious animals that would prey on the weaker fragile animals. When the weaker animals stayed in the pack with the other animals, they were protected and safe. But when the weaker animal got off by himself, he was in the open for his predators to devour him. That is the way it is when a Christian backslides and removes himself from the protection of God and gets in the open as a target for Satan to devour him.

Not only does the backslider put himself in danger, but he also puts his family and friends in jeopardy as well.

We learn by Jonah's example that others are affected when we rebel against God. When God is trying to get the attention of a backslider, it affects everyone around him that includes family, friends, coworkers, and even complete strangers. The storm that God sent because of Jonah put everyone on the ship in danger.

Growing up I remember there was a deacon in the church where I attended. He had a lovely wife and three beautiful children. He was a devoted family man and a faithful deacon at church. He had a demanding job, so on the weekends he liked to go out with some of his friends just to relax. It started off with the guys just hanging out watching sports together. Then eventually they started playing cards. At first they were playing for fun, but then they started playing for cash. One of his friends convinced him and the rest of the guys to go to a casino. Over time he became addicted to gambling. He eventually lost everything that he owned including his home, his cars, and eventually his family. He destroyed his relationship with his family but most importantly with God. I will never forget the impact that backsliding had on his family and on our church family.

When a Christian backslides, he is out of the will of God. God has a perfect plan for each of his children that he wants to perform in their lives. Jeremiah 29:11 says *"For I know the thoughts that I think toward you, saith the Lord, thoughts of peace and not of evil, to give you an expected end"*. God makes his will for our lives known to us. So when you are aware of God's will for your life and you purposely walk outside of his will, then you are treading on dangerous grounds. When you walk outside of the will of God, you are walking outside of his hedge of protection for your life.

It is terrible to never have known the love of Jesus Christ, but it is much worse to have experienced His love and then turned away. Jesus said in St. Luke 9:62, *"No man, having put his hand to the plough, and looking back, is fit for the kingdom"*. God will discipline those who have turned away from him. Deuteronomy 8:5 says "Thou shalt also consider in thine heart that as a man chasteneth his son, so the Lord thy God chasteneth thee". The Bible gives us clear warning about the Lord's chastening and the conviction of the Holy Spirit when a Christian backslides. The Holy Spirit's job is convict the backsliders heart so that he can be restored to right fellowship with the Lord. But it is up to the backslider to heed to these warnings. If the backslider does not heed to these warnings, eventually his heart will hardened and he will not be able to repent. *For it is impossible for those who were once enlightened, and have tasted the heavenly gift, and were made partakers of the Holy Ghost, And have tasted the good word of the Lord, and the powers of the world to come, if they shall fall away, to renew them again unto repentance, seeing they crucify themselves to the Son of God afresh, and put him to open shame*(Hebrews 5:4-6). Those who have known the way of the Lord, and have fallen, and have not repented will come under judgment with the wicked sinners. Isaiah 1:28 says *"And the destruction of the transgressors and of the sinners shall be together and they that forsook the Lord shall be consumed.* Hebrews 10: 26 *"For if we go on sinning willfully after receiving the knowledge of truth, there no longer remains a sacrifice for sins".* If a believer continues to willfully sin, the blood of Christ will no longer protect him from God's judgment. God's anger that he showed toward unbelievers will be unleashed on those who bring the blood of Christ into ridicule and shame. Some Christians have died before their time because they have strayed so far away from God and have become so rebellious that God refused to let them continue to repudiate Jesus' sacrifice.

What are the consequences of backsliding?

As fore mentioned in chapter one, turning away from God is very dangerous and there are penalties that must be paid in doing so. There are several consequences that a backslider may face. One is being rejected by God and cast out of his presence. According to 2 Kings 17th chapter 17-18 verses, God rejected the Israelites and cast them out of his presence because they were serving other gods. Verse 17 says "And they caused their sons and their daughters to pass through the fire and used divination and enchantments, and sold themselves to do evil in the sight of the Lord, to provoke him to anger." Verse 18 says, "Therefore the Lord was very angry with Israel and removed them out of his sight: there was none left but the tribe Judah only. Israel had a history of continual spiritual harlotry. Time and time again God had sent chastisement and His prophets to bring about their repentance and restoration. The Israelites would not heed to his warnings, so God had no other choice but to bring judgment upon them.

The phrase "reprobate mind" is found in Romans 1:28 in reference to those whom God has rejected as godless and wicked. *"And even as they did not like to retain God in their knowledge, God gave them over to a reprobate mind, to do those things which are not convenient".* A reprobate means unapproved, that is, rejected; by implication worthless. People who are classified as having a reprobate mind have some knowledge of God and perhaps know of His commandments. However, they live impure lives and have very little desire to please God. Those who have reprobate minds live corrupt and selfish lives. Sin is justified and acceptable to them. In verse 28, we learn that these people had suppressed the truth by their wickedness and their minds were corrupt concerning the faiths. The reprobates are those whom God has rejected and has left to their own devices.

Proverbs 1:20-33 gives a clear depiction of the danger that surrounds the life of one who has refused to change his ways and turn back to God. It says

> ²⁰*Out in the open wisdom calls aloud,*
> *she raises her voice in the public square;*
>
> ²¹*on top of the wall she cries out,*
> *at the city gate she makes her speech:*
>
> ²²*"How long will you who are simple love your simple ways?*
> *How long will mockers delight in mockery*
> *and fools hate knowledge?*
>
> ²³*Repent at my rebuke!*
> *Then I will pour out my thoughts to you,*
> *I will make known to you my teachings.*
>
> ²⁴*But since you refuse to listen when I call*
> *and no one pays attention when I stretch out my hand,*
>
> ²⁵*since you disregard all my advice*
> *and do not accept my rebuke,*
>
> ²⁶*I in turn will laugh when disaster strikes you;*
> *I will mock when calamity overtakes you—*

²⁷*when calamity overtakes you like a storm,*
when disaster sweeps over you like a whirlwind,
when distress and trouble overwhelm you.

²⁸*"Then they will call to me but I will not answer;*
they will look for me but will not find me,

²⁹*since they hated knowledge*
and did not choose to fear the LORD.

³⁰*Since they would not accept my advice*
and spurned my rebuke,

³¹*they will eat the fruit of their ways*
and be filled with the fruit of their schemes.

³²*For the waywardness of the simple will kill them,*
and the complacency of fools will destroy them;

³³*but whoever listens to me will live in safety*
and be at ease, without fear of harm.

A backslider has two options. One, they can listen to Satan's lies and believe that they have gone too far, made too many mistakes and have been away from God for too long, and just give up. Or they can make the right decision and turn back from sin and enjoy a restored relationship with God. Jonah made the right decision and turned back to God. The bible says that he prayed unto the Lord his God out of the fish's belly and said, *I cried by reason of mine affliction unto the Lord, and he heard me, out of the belly of hell cried I, and thou heardest my voice*(Jonah verse 1&2). God is waiting for you to turn back to him. He is a loving and forgiving God and he will heal you from your backsliding. Jeremiah 3:22 says "*Return, ye backsliding children, and I will heal your backslidings. Behold, we come unto thee: for thou art the Lord our God. Hosea 14:4 says*" *I will heal their backsliding, I will love them freely: for mine anger is turned away from him.*

Discussion Questions

1. What happens when a Christian backslides?

_____

_____

_____

_____

_____

_____

_____

_____

_____

_____

_____

_____

_____

_____

_____

_____

_____

_____

_____

_____

_____

2. What does it mean to have a reprobate mind?

_____

_____

_____

_____

_____

_____

_____

_____

_____

_____

_____

_____

_____

_____

_____

_____

_____

_____

_____

_____

_____

_____

HOW TO KEEP FROM FALLING?

Chapter 6

Now unto him that is able to keep you from falling, and to present you faultless before the presence of his glory with exceeding joy. Jude 1:24

THE KEY TO PREVENT FROM drifting away is to keep your relationship with God as your top priority. Nothing should come before us cultivating an intimate relationship with God. After all that is why we were created, so that should be our main precedence. Often times we set our hearts and minds on trying to achieve goals that will only bring us temporary satisfaction, that we get side tracked and lose focus. It is easy to get off course, when you have everything else above making your relationship with God first. Matthew 6:33 says *Seek ye first the kingdom of God and his righteousness and all these things shall be added unto you.* If you keep your relationship with God as your main priority, you will be able to stay on course.

To combat your chances of falling back into sin, a game plan should be executed. Please rest assure if you do not have a plan, you will inevitable fail again. You will once again be in a position where you are distant in your relationship with God. I know that you don't want that, so let's talk about how you can prepare before you are faced with issues that might pose as a problem for you. While, I don't know what your personal reasons were which caused you to drift from God, I am sure that I can give you a few strategies that you can implement in any situation. All of the strategies that I am giving are based on the Word of God, so I know that they will work if you will only implement them.

1. Be Committed to Daily Fellowship with Jesus Christ.

My husband often says that I am not a morning person, and that I function best at night. Perhaps I might be a little sluggish about getting certain things done in the morning, but one thing that I am adamant about is starting my day in fellowship with God. I have found that I have a much better day when I start my day off with fellowship with God and have a much better sleep when I end my day with God.

But I have heard some people say that morning works best for them, while others say that night works best for them because there are less distractions. Please understand that you can have fellowship with God in heart at any time of the day. There are times throughout my day while I am completing my daily assignments, that I am singing praises to God or will whisper a prayer to him. During those times, I am in fellowship with God, but I still set aside a special time that I can concentrate completely on God and hear His voice. It has been during my committed fellowship time that God has given me a revelation that prove to be pivotal to getting the answer to my prayer and for the getting the instructions for an assignment that God was preparing me for.

Whatever time you designate to spend with God, it should be unhurried, quality time. This should be a time when you are less distracted and can really focus on talking to God and listening to Him as well. Don't consider this time as another thing to do. Spending time with God is not one of the things on your to do list. Although you may have many things on your agenda, you can't get in such a hurry in your daily lives that you forget the most important thing that is spending time with God.

2. Keep God In Your Plans—Sometimes we tend to leave God out of the simple things in life. We leave him out of the things that we think that we can handle on our own, but chose to seek

49

him during the tough times. God wants to be in every detail of your life. When you leave God out of your plans and daily affairs, then sin has an opportunity to enter in your life. My friend, sin is more than a three-letter word. It is very powerful and can lead to destruction. Sin will take you down a path that you never intended to go and it will cost you more than you ever intended to pay. You must keep God first place in your life. We keep him first by seeking Him. And you can't do that and be a lazy Christian but you must exert consistent effort and keep him on the front burner. Over and over again, the Bible tells us we must seek God first and foremost if we want His blessing in our lives. To seek means to go after with intense effort". You can't be a lazy Christian and seek God when it is convenient for you. When put God on the back burner, you are more likely to drift away from God.

3. **Stay In the Word of God**—God's word is to our soul as physical food is to our body. We have to eat our physical food on a daily basis in order to stay healthy. We don't eat at the beginning of the week with the expectation that we will be full for the rest of the week. The word of God is our spiritual food. Just as we eat our physical food to stay healthy, we must eat our spiritual food to stay spiritually healthy. It is not enough to go to church on Sunday and listen to a preacher's sermon and expect to get enough spiritual food to last you all week.

   As believers we must stay rooted and grounded in God's word. We have to keep studying and learning daily. God is not concerned with how fast you can read through his word, and unless he has given you a specific passage of scripture to read, it really does not matter if you read 1 chapter or 5 chapters a day. What is important is that we hear what we read with our spiritual ears, and meditate on what we have read so it can penetrate our hearts. I believe that God would much prefer that you read one verse and get a revelation, than to read a whole chapter and miss what he is saying to you.

4. **Stay In Fellowship with Other Believers**—You can't make it alone as a Christian. We need the strength and prayers of other believers. It also helps to have other believers to hold you accountable to staying on course with living a Godly and holy

life. (Hebrews 10:25) says "Not forsaking the assembling of ourselves together, as the manner of some is: but exhorting one another: and so much the more, as ye see the day approaching".

5. **Stand Firm in Your Faith.** Difficult times will come in our lives, but we must stand firm in our faith. We can not waver in our faith. Galatians 5:1 says "It is for freedom that Christ has set us free. Stand firm then and do not let yourselves be burdened again by a yoke of slavery. Jesus tells us in John 16:33 that we are going to have tribulations. He says *"These things I have spoken unto you, that in me ye might have peace. In the world ye shall have tribulation: but be of good cheer, I have overcome the world"*. As Christians we will have trials and tribulations, but we must stand firm in our faith. We must keep believing in the Word of God and believing that God is going to do exactly what he said he will. Often times when things get hard, Christians get discouraged when they are faced with trials. I preached a sermon entitled "Going Through A Test—Will you Pass or Fail? In the sermon I talked about the choice that we each have to make whether we will pass or fail our test. We can pass our test by choosing to operate in faith and trust God or we can make the choice to operate in fear, doubt God and fail the test.

6. **Live A Disciplined Life**—A part of living a disciplined life is being committed to reading your Bible, spending quality time with God and praying. Our flesh is not inclined to pray, read God's Word or seek His face. These things take discipline. We have to bring ourselves under subjection to do them. We have to make spending time with God our top priority. The very moment that we set our hearts to seek God, Satan will send a conspiracy of interruptions designed to keep us from fellowshipping with God. We have to be committed to seeking God.

   Another aspect of living a life that is well disciplined is the having the dedication to follow God's will. Our dedication to God's will is an act of surrender or submission. When we seek to discern the will of God we must be committed to doing the will as it is revealed in the Word of God(John 7:17).

7. **Take Responsibility for Your Thoughts**—One essential key to staying on course with your walk with God is to take responsibility

of your thought life. God has given us the power to take authority over our own thoughts. Phillipians 4:8 says "Finally, brethren, whatsoever things are true, whatsoever things are honest, whatsoever things are just, whatsoever things are pure, whatsoever things are lovely, whatsoever things are of good report; if there be any virtue, and if there be any praise, think on these things. These are the things that we should set our minds on. Romans 12:1-2 says "I beseech you therefore, brethren, by the mercies of God, that ye present your bodies a living sacrifice, holy, acceptable unto God, which is your reasonable service. And be not conformed to this world: but be ye transformed by the renewing of your mind, that ye may prove what is that good, and acceptable, and perfect, will of God". To be conformed to the world means to follow and pattern ourselves after it. Before conversion, we lived according to the world system, its philosophies, values and lifestyle that was opposed to God. We were controlled by the spirit of the world and walked in total disobedience, gratifying the cravings of our sinful nature and following after its desires and thoughts. But because of God's mercy and love, we were given a new life. A new life which entails having the mind of Christ. 1 Corinthians 2:16 says "For who hath known the mind of the Lord, that he may instruct him? But we have the mind of Christ".

It is essential that we renew our minds with the Word of God and to come against anything that does not line up with the Word of God. 2 Corinthians 10:5 says "Casting down imaginations, and every high thing that exalteth itself against the knowledge of God, and bringing into captivity every thought to the obedience of Christ". Satan will try to build strongholds in our minds, but we have weapons to fight against him. Whenever a thought enters our mind that is contrary to what the Word of God says we must engage in spiritual war and bring it under subjection. We must careful what we feed our souls because what we feed our souls is what we will meditate on.

8. **Watch the Company That You Keep** Friends are very important to have and we all need them. Your friends should draw you closer to God rather than away from Him. If a person tempts you to do the wrong thing then you don't need to be with that person.

1 Corinthians 15:33 says *"**Do not be deceived: Evil company corrupts good habits**".*

I had a friend who had a drug addiction to cocaine. She went to rehab and was doing well and on her way to recovery. She was back in church and was serving the Lord. She was doing good until her friends or "so called friends" enticed her to come back to the streets. She started smoking cocaine again. As long as she associated with the people in the church who loved and cared about her, she did not smoke, but as soon as she started hanging with her "friends" she went back to her old habits.

In order to keep from falling you must break all ungodly ties. A Christian should live a holy life that reflects the nature of God. He should separate himself from actions, influences or people that will contaminate him. 2 Corinthians 6:14-18 says "Be ye not unequally yoked together with unbelievers: for what fellowship hath righteousness with unrighteousness? and what communion hath light with darkness?

¹⁵And what concord hath Christ with Belial? or what part hath he that believeth with an infidel?

¹⁶And what agreement hath the temple of God with idols? for ye are the temple of the living God; as God hath said, I will dwell in them, and walk in them; and I will be their God, and they shall be my people.

¹⁷Wherefore come out from among them, and be ye separate, saith the Lord, and touch not the unclean thing; and I will receive you.

¹⁸And will be a Father unto you, and ye shall be my sons and daughters, saith the Lord Almighty.

9. **Avoid Temptation**-One of the key strategies that is very beneficial in staying on course with your relationship with God, is avoiding temptation. Temptation occurs when the opportunity is presented to do what we know is wrong, whether against God, others or ourselves. Everyone faces temptation at one time or another in his or her life. Being tempted is not wrong, it is when we give in to temptation that it turns into sin. But we don't have to give in to the temptation. 1 Corinthians 10:13 says *"There hath no temptation taken you but such as is common to man: but God*

is faithful, who will not suffer you to be tempted above that ye are able, but will with the temptation also make a way of escape that ye may be able to bear it". I am reminded of the story of Joseph and Potiphar's wife. Joseph was a righteous man, and the Lord blessed him. When Potiphar saw that Joseph was blessed by God and was successful in everything that he did, he appointed him as overseer. This meant that Joseph was responsible for Potiphar's house and everything that he owned. Potiphar's wife was attracted to Joseph because he was handsome.

She tried to tempt Joseph by asking him to lie with her. But Joseph refused. Day after day she would ask Joseph to lie with her. But Joseph always refused. One day when Joseph went into the house to take care of his responsibilities, none of the men who worked in the house were there. When Potiphar's wife saw that she was alone with Joseph, she grabbed a hold of his cloak(coat), and tried to coax him to come to her. Joseph pulled away and ran, leaving her holding his cloak. Potiphar's wife called the men of the house and showed them his cloak. She told them that Joseph had tried to have sex with her, but she screamed. After she screamed, Joseph ran away. Of course this was not true. Joseph refused to give in to his temptation. He used wisdom in his decision to run from her and as a result he avoided yielding to temptation.

If you ever in a situation like Joseph, what will be your plan of action? I hope that you will do what Joseph did and run away. Don't be afraid or ashamed to run from temptation, no matter what others may say about you. Most importantly, don't put yourself in the position where you would be tempted. If you are in a relationship that is hindering your walk with the Lord, then you need to reestablish the boundaries of your relationship. If your temptation deals with you watching pornography, stay off the computer, and ask God to help you! If someone in your life is the problem with you being fully committed to God, then you need to get that person out of your life. Nobody is worth you losing out on being in a loving relationship with the Lord.

10. **Search Your Heart**—The words found in Lamentations 3:40 "Let us search and try our ways, and turn again to the Lord is a good

starting point to guard against falling back into sin. It is important that we search our lives to see what has the potential to cause us to stray away from God or what has already caused us to stray. You need to search your ways and identify the activities that you have engaged in and the thoughts that you have allowed to take captive over your mind. What has been lacking in your spiritual life? What habits do you have that have crowded God out of his proper place? What temptation you have succumbed too in the past that has weakened your testimony? What unconfessed sins do you have harboring in your heart subjecting yourself to the potential of having a spiritual heart attack? Once you have searched your heart you will begin to understand the root cause of your problem. You will also able to identify the issues that have the potential to strain your relationship with God.

11. **Recharge Your Battery**-I had the distinct honor of accompanying my husband on his Governor for Georgia campaign in 2010. A task of this magnitude required that we traveled great distances to attend various events. It was customary for me to take several pictures of my husband as he spoke during each of his engagements. Among the many events that I attended with him, there is one occasion that I probably won't ever forget. In my haste in helping him get prepared for one of his events, I forgot to do one important thing. As my husband stood to give his speech, I positioned myself so I could take his picture. I took two pictures of him, and was in the process of taking the third picture, when I noticed that the red light was on. It was then that I realized that I had forgotten to charge the battery on the camera. I was able to take two more pictures before the battery was completely dead in my camera. I was very disappointed that I was not able to take any more pictures, as I am sure that you can imagine. Just when I needed my camera the most it could not perform the task that I needed it too because I had not done my part in charging the batteries.

As Christians we must take the responsibility and do our part to keep our spiritual batteries charged up. We keep our spiritual batteries charged with the Word of God, prayer, fasting and by staying connected to our power source, which is the Holy

Ghost. Acts 1:8 says "But ye shall receive power, after that the Holy Ghost is come upon you: and ye shall be witnesses unto me both in Jerusalem, and in all Judea and in Samaria, and unto the uttermost part of the earth. The Holy Ghost gives us the power that we need to live a holy life and to remain in intimate fellowship with God. Our total dependence on the Holy Ghost will keep our spiritual batteries charged, but if we fail to rely on his power we are destined to fail. We can't afford to disconnect from our power source.

Implementing these strategies will better prepare you to avoid the pitfalls that cause you to fall back into a world of sin.

Discussion Questions

1. What are some strategies that you can use to keep from falling into sin?

_____

_____

_____

_____

_____

_____

_____

_____

_____

_____

_____

_____

_____

_____

_____

_____

_____

_____

_____

_____

_____

_____

_____

2. What areas of sin are you struggling in?

_____

_____

_____

_____

_____

_____

_____

_____

_____

_____

_____

_____

_____

_____

_____

_____

_____

_____

_____

_____

_____

_____

_____

TURNING BACK TO GOD

Chapter 7

If my people, which are called by my name, shall humble themselves, and pray, and seek my face, and turn from their wicked ways; then will I hear from heaven, and will forgive their sin, and will heal their land. 2Chronicles 7:14

G OD CHOSE THE ISRAELITES TO be his chosen people above all people that were upon the face of the earth. According to Deuteronomy 6:7, God did not chose the Israelites because they were great in number, because actually they were the fewest in number, but God chose them because of His special love for them. He demonstrated just how much he loved them when they were taken into slavery and held in bondage under the deceptive and conniving leadership of Pharaoh, king of Egypt.

In a previous chapter, we discussed the love affair between God and the Israelites, but I think that it is important to revisit the topic and address some of the things that took place during Israel's time of bondage that emphasized God's compassion, mercy and love that he has for the Israelites. We will begin our discussion with addressing why the Israelites were in slavery. In the book of Exodus chapter 1, we are given the account of how and why the Israelites were in slavery. After the death of Joseph, a new king was over Egypt. It was apparent that this king felt that the Israelites opposed a threat to him and his people because of what he said recorded in verses 9 and 10. He said to his people,*" Behold the people of the children of Israel are more and mightier than we: Come on, let us deal wisely with them; lest they multiply and it come to pass, that, when there falleth out any war, they join also unto their enemies, and fight against us, and so get them up out of the land".* Because of Pharaoh's fear that the Israelites would join forces with his enemies in the event of a war, he devised a plan to get the Israelites out the land. To carry out this plan, he assigned taskmasters over the children of Israel to afflict them with their burdens. But the more they afflicted the Israelites, the more they multiplied and grew. This grieved the Egyptians, so in an act of retaliation, they made the children of Israel serve with rigor. In verse 14, it says *"And they made their lives bitter with hard bondage, in mortar, in brick, and in all manner of service in the field: all their service, wherein they made them serve, was with rigor".*

Pharaoh gave a commandment to the midwives, that when they helped the Hebrew women during childbirth, to kill the child, if it was a son, and to let the child live, if it was a daughter. Because of their fear (reverence) of God, they did not follow through as Pharaoh had commanded. Questioned by him for their disobedience to his command, the midwives told him that the Hebrew women were not as the Egyptian women in that they were fast, and had already delivered before they had gotten there. Because of their faithfulness to God, God provided households for them. Determined to execute his plan, Pharaoh then commanded all his people saying "Every son that is born ye shall cast into the river and every daughter ye shall save alive".

Now Exodus Chapter 2 introduces to us a prominent character who God uses to help the Israelites while they are in slavery. Call it mother's intuition or a divine revelation from God himself, but Moses' mother knew that there was something special about him. She hid him for three months, but when she could no longer hide him, she implemented a plan to save his life. She got a papyrus basket for him and coated it with tar and pitch. Then she placed Moses in it and put it among the reeds along the bank of the Nile river.

I like the next part of the story because to me it gives a clear indication that this was a plan orchestrated by God. When Pharaoh's daughter went down to the Nile to bathe, she saw the basket that Moses was in. She sent her slave girl to get the basket. While opening the basket, she saw baby Moses and had compassion on him. Pharaoh's daughter sent for one of the Hebrew woman to nurse the baby. The woman who was chosen was Moses biological mother. Pharaoh's daughter told her to nurse the baby and she would pay her. She nursed the baby until he was of age, and then she gave him back to Pharaoh's daughter.

Although Moses escaped the clutches of Pharaoh as an infant, he faced an attempt on his life later on. When Moses witnessed an Egyptian beating a Hebrew, he killed the Egyptian and hid him in the sand. Pharaoh heard about this and tried to kill Moses. He fled and went to live in Midian.

Recognizing the fact that Moses had a special calling on his life, we find in Exodus chapter 3 the special assignment that God had for him to do. God used the illustration of the burning bush to get the attention of Moses. Moses' assignment was to bring the Israelites out of Egypt. Like some of us do sometimes when we think that God has called us to do a special assignment that we feel we are not equipped to carry out, Moses questioned God. His response to God gives a clear indication that he felt this way when he said "Who am I, that I should go to Pharaoh and bring the Israelites out of Egypt". God reassured Moses that he would be with him, and he even gave him a sign to reinforce his assurance; he said "when you have brought the people out of Egypt, you will worship God on this mountain".

Moses still not convinced that he is the man for the job, he imposed a question to God; "suppose I go to the Israelites and say to them, The God of your fathers have sent me to you and they ask me "what is his name? Then what shall I tell them? God told Moses, "tell them I AM sent you.".

With one more attempt to convince God, Moses said "What if they don't believe me or listen to me or say "The Lord did not appear to you? This time God used a different approach for Moses. He gave Moses a demonstration so that he could have proof that he had appeared to him. The first miracle that God performed was changing the staff in Moses hand into a snake. He told Moses to throw the staff on the ground and the staff turned into a snake, and then he changed the snake back into a staff. The second illustration God used was when he told Moses to put his hand inside his cloak, Moses did.

He took his hand out of his cloak and it was leprous like snow. God then told Moses to put his leprous hand back into his cloak and take it back out. When he took it out, it was white as snow. It was restored like the rest of his flesh. God told Moses if they don't believe the first, then maybe they will believe the second miracle. But just in case, here is a third-take the water from the Nile River and pour it on dry ground. The water will become blood.

You would think that that would be enough to reassure Moses, but he still came with an excuse about the lack of his ability to speak well. Moses said "I have never been an eloquent speaker. I am slow of speech and tongue". God gave Moses a reminder that he was the one who gave him his mouth.

Finally Moses got to the point and said what he probably really wanted to say all along, "Please send someone else to do it". Let me stop here for a moment and ask you a question "Has God given you an assignment that you felt that you were not equipped to do? Have you drifted away from that assignment? Let me encourage you to do what God has called you to do. If God has given you the task of completing a mission, be reassured that God will be with you until the end. Philippians 1:6 says "Being confident of this very thing, that he hath begun a good work in you will perform it until the day of Jesus Christ".

Now back to the story. God was angry with Moses. He told Moses to take his brother Aaron with him and he would be with both of them. The Bible teaches us that Moses and Aaron went to Pharaoh to give the command that God had given them: "let my people go". Each time that Moses and Aaron went to Pharaoh God hardened Pharaoh's heart, and he would not let the Israelites go. Because he would not listen, God sent 10 plagues; plague of blood, plague of frogs, plague of gnats, plague of lice, plague of flies, plague of cattle, plague of boils, and plague of darkness(Read Exodus 7-10)

In Exodus 12th chapter verses 31-37, Pharaoh commanded Moses and Aaron to leave Egypt. The children of Israel journeyed from Rameses to Succoth, about six hundred thousand on foot that were men, beside children. God led the children of Israel through the wilderness and performed many miracles on their behalf; the parting of the Red Sea, the pillar of cloud and fire to guide them, the manna from heaven, the water from the rocks, the appearance and voice of Almighty God on Mount Sinai, and the defeat of their enemies. He told them that he was going to bring them into safe cities, put them in good homes and shower them with good things. They would have wells they wouldn't have to dig and vineyards they wouldn't have to plant.

Although God had performed these miracles for them, they still fell into the trap of serving idol gods. They were quick to forget the Lord and what he had done for them. They complained and murmured even though God was taking care of them. They even put God to the test to see if he was able to do the things that he said that he would do. They turned their back on the only true living God. They forsook the very God who delivered them from slavery, and served idol gods. Judges 2:13 says" And they forsook the Lord, and served Baal and Ashtaroth".

As we read throughout the book of Judges, we find that they repeatedly turned their back on God. Judges 2:11 says "The children of Israel did evil in the sight of the Lord. They had established a pattern of sinning against God, being rescued by God, then turning away from God again. Everytime the people fell into sin and idolatry, the Lord came back and raised up a judge(leader) to rescue them and set them back on the proper course. God was not obligated to keep raising judges for the Israelites, because they were the ones who broke the covenant and turned their backs on him, but because of God's grace, mercy, faithfulness and His love, he continued to rescue them.

In Judges chapter 10, we find a different course of action taking place. God sold the Israelites into the hands of Philistines and into the hands of the children of Ammon. The Philistines and the children of Ammon held them in oppression for 18 years. Being harassed and left in severe distress led the Israelites to cry out the Lord, saying "We have sinned against thee, both because we have forsaken our God, and also served Baalim". But God had reached a point where he was not as quick to grant forgiveness and deliverance to the Israelites. He brought to their remembrance about how he had delivered them from their enemies several times. He sent this reminder in a form of a question, "And the Lord said unto the children of Israel, Did not I deliver you from the Egyptians, and from the Amorites, from the children of Ammon, and from the Philistines. Yet ye have forsaken me, and served other gods, wherefore I will not deliver you no more". God then issues the Israelites a challenge and told them to cry out the gods that they had chosen to follow and let them deliver them this time.

Responding out desperation, the Israelites offered God a plea, that he would do whatever seemed fitting to Him, if he would only deliver them from their oppressors. They were willing to be punished by God if that is what he deemed necessary. They knew in their hearts that they had sinned against God, and now they are ready to offer him a sincere confession. They have become repentant of the sins that they have committed. They demonstrated true repentance by removing the foreign gods from the midst and began to serve the Lord again.

My friend, you can turn back to God and make a commitment to follow him again. Just like the Israelites, you can get back on track and start serving God again. Despite all of Israel's unfaithfulness, God was moved with compassion for them and forgave them of their sin. The Israelites returned to their rightful position as being obedient children of God, ready and willing to do his will. Are you ready and willing to do God's will again? Isn't it time for you to turn back to God? God is waiting to take you back, if only you will turn back.

To embark on this journey back to God, you must take action. 2 Chronicles 7:14, one of the most quoted scriptures from the Word of God, highlights the instructions on how to get back to God. God promises to both forgive and heal those who have backslide, but that promise is contingent on the action of the backslider. The backslider must play a key role in their efforts to reaching their destiny back to God by humbling themselves, praying, seeking God's face, and turning from their wicked ways. To be humble means to be meek or modesty in behavior, attitude or spirit: not arrogant or prideful. Being humble is essential to turning back to God, but many people who have turned away from God, find it hard to be humble because of a devastating sin called pride. Pride is the opposite of humility. It is oftentimes the root cause of a person backsliding putting him or her in the position where they refuse to acknowledge God and their dependence on Him. They believe that their ways are more important than God's way. The Bible gives us warning about being pride.

Proverbs 16:18 says "pride goes before destruction, a haughty spirit before a fall". According to James 4: 6 God resists the proud, but he gives grace to the humble. God is calling the backslider back to a state of humility. 1Peter 5:6 says Humble yourselves under the mighty hand of God that he may exalt you in due time. When you humble yourself before God you are coming under subjection to God and His authority. You no longer have the desire to live for yourself but rather you want him to be Lord of your life once again. Your focus is not on your agenda and what you want to accomplish, but you are in pursuit of what God wants.

Prayer is the 2nd course of action on your path leading back to God. Prayer is the intimate communication between you and God. It is the mechanism that ushers you into the presence of God. Entering into God's presence, allows you to gain access to His grace. My friend, if you have backslidden and are out of the ark of safety, then you need His grace.

God gives us a promise in James 4:6 "God gives greater grace to those who humble themselves and pray.

Seeking God's face is the next step in reaching your place back in God. To seek God's face, really means you are seeking His heart and mind. You are seeking His way of doing things instead of doing things your way. You are entering into His presence so that the Holy Spirit will reveal to you what in your life is displeasing to God.

Finally, you must turn away from your wicked ways. Turning away from your wicked ways simply is laying down the sin that is in your life. Hebrews 12:1 says, *"Wherefore seeing we also are compassed about with so great a cloud of witnesses, let us lay aside every weight, and the sin which doth so easily beset us, and let us run with patience the race that is set before us"*. Whatever habit, addiction or sin of any kind must be let go of in order to come back to God. Remember sin is what caused you to drift in the first place, so it is understandable that you can not come back to God in that same condition. You must let go of your old ways and make a decision to surrender to God. You lay down your life in the flesh. Paul stated, "I die daily".(1 Corinthians 15:31). Each time that your flesh rises up and attempts to draw you away from God's will you must reject it. God won't enter back into a covenant relationship with you until you have died to your flesh.

Turning back may not be an easy thing to do, but it is necessary. God does not want any of His children to perish but if you do not turn back to Him, that will be your outcome. You do not know when your life will end, that is why you can not delay your time to come back to God. You have held on to your way of doing things long enough. Why don't you accept God's promise to forgive you from your sins now? Don't wait until you hit rock bottom turn back to God.

Discussion Questions

1. What are the steps to turning back to God?

_____

_____

_____

_____

_____

_____

_____

_____

_____

_____

_____

_____

_____

_____

_____

_____

_____

_____

_____

_____

_____

_____

_____

_____

A TURNING POINT EXPERIENCE

Chapter 8

And when he came to himself, he said, How many hired servants of my father's have bread enough and to spare, and I perish with hunger! Luke 15:17

THERE CAN BE MANY DEFINITIONS of the phrase "turning point". A turning point can be viewed from different perspectives depending upon the context of its usage. According to the American Heritage College Dictionary, a turning point is defined as the point at which a significant change or a decisive moment occurs. It is when an action or an event takes a turn for the better or for the worse, or changes in a different direction. I can remember one of my son's basketball games. In the first quarter, they started off being lax and not really exerting the necessary energy that they needed to dominate their opponents. The second quarter, they made a lot of careless mistakes which allowed the other team to steal the ball and score points. Our team was losing by more than 10 points. The third quarter rolled around, and in the beginning it was much of the same thing; our boys made careless mistakes, not exerting enough energy to get rebounds, the referee blowing the whistle and giving hand signals for double dribbling violations and on occasion for fouling their opponents. Pretty soon the coach for our team called a time out and pulled our boys to the side to give them a pep talk in hopes to change the course of things. It was the second half of the third quarter that things begin to change. The second half of the third quarter was definitely a lot different than the first half. Our boys were refreshed and rejuvenated. They had reached a turning point and had begun to implement all the drills and skills that they needed to dominate on the court. I must say that at first it didn't seem that things would turn out in our teams favor, but it did. Our team defeated their opponents and won the game.

A turning point is when you reach a stage in your life where you make the decision that something must change and you are not going back to the way things were. When you reach a turning point, you have come to the conclusion that enough is enough and change is inevitable.

Allow me to share a story about my friend's turning point. Angie accepted Jesus into her heart at a very early age. She loved the Lord and did everything that she could to please him. She was active in all of the youth programs in her local church. Angie was a wonderful example for the young adults to follow. As time went on and she grew older she got involved in more school activities. This left little time for her church activities. She started talking to some of the other teenage girls who were not a part of her church group. They started to persuade her to do things that were not Godly. Eventually her attitude about God began to change. She justified it by saying, "I may not go to church as much as I used to but I still love God in my own way". Angie slowly started to drift away from everything that she knew and forgot all about God. She was headed in the wrong direction. She started smoking pot and drinking. It started off being her "weekend" thing, but overtime she used drugs every day.

Later Angie met a guy who she thought was her knight in shining armor. He meant the world to her. Their relationship grew until eventually they got married. The first two years were good, but things started to change in their relationship. Angie found out that her husband had not been faithful. They soon got a divorce. This devastated her. She was at the lowest point in her life. She started to think about how her life was when she was younger in church and serving the Lord. She thought unlike her husband, how faithful Jesus had been to her. She realized that she needed Jesus in her life. Angie finally decided to turn around and recommit her life to Jesus.

Life often has many turning points; some of which are more significant than others. We each have our own perception about what represents a turning point in our lives. For example, suppose there is a job opening at a local grocery store for the position of cashier. A 17 year old applies for the position, as does a 45 year old mother of four children. In the eyes of the 17 year old, reaching this milestone of getting hired for her very first job, allows her the independence and freedom to buy the latest fashion, or to upgrade to the newest cell phone.

Whereas the mother of 4, who has the responsibility of taking care of her children, may have a totally different view about getting the job. After struggling month after month trying to make ends meet, this mother may view getting hired for this job as the end of her financial struggle because she now has the means to provide for her children. This might not be a major turning point in the life of the teenager, but to the single mom of four who has been struggling to make ends meet each month, having a job can make the difference between whether she has food to feed her children or not. In this illustration, having a job may have more significance to the mom rather than the teenager. I am certainly not saying that the job is not important to the teenager or that it is not beneficial to him or her. But I am saying that having the job can be a turning point in both the life of the teenager and the mother, but for different reasons. The teenager might view having a job as something to do in his or her spare time whereas the mother might view it as an opportunity to sustain life and turn her financial situation around. This would prove to be a critical turning point in her life.

Any transition or significant change in life can serve as a catalyst for a turning point. It could be something as serious as being diagnosed with a disease which might would serve as a catalyst to change your eating and exercise habits or it could be getting a divorce from your spouse, of the death of a love one.

I know from personal experience that the death of a love one can definitely be a turning point in a person's life. In 2007, my mother was diagnosed with state 4 colon cancer. Sadly, she passed away on May 4, 2008. My life changed significantly. Life has not been the same since her death. My mother was the glue that held our family together. She was the one who kept the family together living in harmony and peace. She touched so many lives and led some many people to Christ, by spreading the Word of God and by her living example. My mother's death was a turning point in not only my life, but in my dad's and my three sisters as well. We all had to learn to live life without having my mom and her guidance. I personally had to adjust to not being able to call her and ask her advice on a certain situations or not being able to tell her about the latest thing that my kids were involved in. This was a major change in my life.

As I fore mentioned, getting a divorce can also be a turning point in a person's life. Unfortunately, I witnessed the devastation that my friend experienced as she and her husband went through a divorce. After many years of being single, she had finally met the man of her dreams. In the beginning of the relationship, things were going great. They were in love with each other and got along well with each other. It was not until they were faced with financial obligations that trouble in their relationship began. They began to have continuous arguments about money; who was spending what and where. The problems escalated until it reached a point where they both decided that it would be best if they went their separate ways. They eventually got a divorce. This left my friend in a desperate situation. Suddenly she was on her own. She no longer had her husband to depend on to take care of her and provide for her. This was a major turning point in her life.

A turning point does not have to be that drastic. Turning points do not have to be negative. There are some positive turning points that we will experience in life. Most teenagers look forward to getting their driving license and driving for the first time. A student transitioning from the high school level to college level can viewed as a turning point. The decision to change careers can also be a turning point in a person's life.

Marriage can also be a turning point in a person's life. After dating for only two months, my husband asked me to marry him. We were engaged for a total of ten months and on May 11, 1991 we were married. Except for the short time that I had lived on a college campus, I had always lived with my parents so it was a bit of an adjustment now living with my husband. I moved from a city with a population of about 15,000 to a city with a population of about 1000.

In the beginning that was a challenge, but over time I got accustomed to the small town.

I was accustomed to living a single life, as was he, not really having to answer to anyone. When I was single I was not responsible for anyone except myself. I could do things the way I wanted, when I wanted, and how I wanted. But that all changed when I got married. I had to begin to think differently and not just about myself, but now I had a spouse who I had to consider when I made decisions. As with any relationship, there were some issues that had to be ironed out, but for the most part married life was good.

Another turning point in my life was when I had our first child. After going through 3 years of not being able to get pregnant, having to take medication and eventually having surgery, I can definitely tell you it was a turning point in my life when I found out that I was finally pregnant. I don't think I will ever be able to put in words the joy that I felt when I heard the doctor say "Mrs. Camon, you are pregnant".

After our son Carl Jr. was born, our lives were no longer the same. As any parent will tell you, having a baby will change your life forever. Sleepless nights, diaper changes and early AM feedings come with the territory of being a parent of a newborn. I am proud to have say, that I had the opportunity and privilege of being the parent of four newborns; Carl Jr., Aaron, Camille and Candace. Both getting married and having my babies, brought about a change. It was a change that I gladly welcomed.

Although getting married and becoming a parent brought me so much joy, they don't compare to the joy that I had when I accepted Jesus in my heart. I grew up in a Christian home where I was encouraged to trust Jesus as my Savior. Even at a young age, I felt a void in my life that I knew that could only be filled by God. Accepting Jesus into my heart was the most important turning point in my life.

We all undergo changes in our lives that lead to turning point experiences. Sometimes it is difficult changes of lifetime habits that lead us to a turning point in our lives. Unfortunately some of us reach our turning point only after we have hit rock bottom. Hitting rock bottom is often associated with a person who has an addiction to drugs or alcohol, but there are other areas in our lives that we can hit rock bottom. We can also have a spiritual downfall in our lives. Although God loves us, sometimes he will allow us hit a spiritual wall, letting us go as far as we can go on our own strength. Then we can realize that we can't make it without Him. I think that the story of the prodigal son recorded in Luke 15th chapter accurately illustrates that point. In this story there is a man who had two sons. The younger son asked his father for his inheritance. Typically, a son would receive his inheritance at the time of his father's death. The fact that son asked his father for inheritance early, shows his rebellion and lack of respect that he had for his father.

The father granted him his request and his son went to a far country. He wasted his inheritance on extravagant living. Many people are like the prodigal son, they want to get as far away from God as possible, but they want their inheritance too. They want their blessings, but they do not want the blessor.

When he had spent all that he had, a famine came and he was now living in lack. Out of desperation, he took a job feeding pigs. This was degrading for him because pigs were unclean animals, and Jews normally did not touch pigs. So for the son to take this job, this is a sure indication that he was at his lowest point. It was the fact that he has lost everything, all of his friends had abandoned him, and he was so hungry that he was willing to eat what the pigs ate, that led him to his turning point experience. After reaching his lowest point and hitting rock bottom, he finally came to his senses. In verse 17 he says "And when he came to himself, he said, How many hired servants of my father's have bread enough and to spare, and I perish with hunger"! I believe he was saying "I know that what I did was wrong, I might have even disappointed my father, but now I've come to the point where I realize my mistake and I want to get it right with my father". He realized that his father was in the position to help him, so he must get back in connection with his father even if it meant that he had to be a hired servant.

My friend, we all have experiences in life. Some are good and some are bad. Each of us have made a decision and chosen a path that has led us to the position where we are today. Perhaps the decisions that you have made have led you down a path of destruction and now you are living a life that is not pleasing in the eyesight of God. You may have made promises to yourself, to your family and friends and most importantly to God, that you would change and get back on the right path, but yet you continue to make the same mistakes over and over again. Let me encourage you not to give up. All is not lost; you can have a new beginning in Christ. If you are in the position, where you have allowed short lived escapades to cause you to drift away from God then you need to come back to God. You may be at your lowest point and feel that you can't get back up again. You may feel that there is not any hope for you, but that could not more farther from the truth. No matter what you are facing, there is hope for you in Jesus. The blood of Jesus can cleanse any sin that you have committed, mend any broken relationship, and has the power to overcome any addiction that you have. Isn't it time for you to reach a turning point in your life and head in the right direction?

If you are tired of living the life that you are living. If you are ready to experience the greatest turning point in your life, then I encourage you to pray this prayer with me:

Lord Jesus, I acknowledge that I have drifted from you. I ask that you forgive me and cleanse me from all unrighteousness. I want to experience the greatest turning point and restore my relationship with you. I love you.

Reflection

1. In your own words, describe what a turning point experience is?

_____

_____

_____

_____

_____

_____

_____

_____

_____

_____

_____

_____

_____

_____

_____

_____

_____

_____

_____

_____

_____

_____

_____

2. What were the circumstances that caused the prodigal son to reach his turning point?

_____

_____

_____

_____

_____

_____

_____

_____

_____

_____

_____

_____

_____

_____

_____

_____

_____

_____

_____

_____

_____

3. How does the life of a backslidden Christian relate to the life of the prodigal son?

_____

_____

_____

_____

_____

_____

_____

_____

_____

_____

_____

_____

_____

_____

_____

_____

_____

_____

_____

_____

_____

_____

_____

4. Discuss the importance of a backslidden Christian reaching a turning point in his or her life.

_____

_____

_____

_____

_____

_____

_____

_____

_____

_____

_____

_____

_____

_____

_____

_____

_____

_____

_____

_____

_____

_____

COME BACK HOME

Chapter 9

I will arise and go to my father, and will say to him Father, I have sinned against heaven and before you. Luke 15:18

IN THE PREVIOUS CHAPTER, WE learned that the prodigal son had sinned against both God and his father. He had indulged in riotous living and now was in need of forgiveness. At this venture in his life, he had two choices that he could have made. The first being, he could have felt that he had done so much wrong that he was not worthy of forgiveness, and continued to live in sin. Secondly, he could reach a turning point in his life and realize that he although he made mistakes, he could seek his father's forgiveness and come back home to his father. Thank God he did just that. He made the decision that he was not going to stay in the position that he was in. Even if it meant being in the position of his father's hired servant.

Often times when a Christian finds himself in fault, they won't do anything about it. They choose to stay in the sinful position that they are in, and continue to drift further and further away from the Lord. I have heard many people say "you might have fallen into the pig pin, but that doesn't mean you have to wallow in the mud". That simply means just because you have made a mistake does not mean that you have to continue to make the same mistake and continue to live in sin. You can get back up again. Just like that prodigal son you can come to your senses, realize your mistakes, repent and come back home.

Before the son even made it home, the father saw him, had compassion, ran and fell on his neck and kissed him. The fact that the father was able to see his son from a distance, indicates that perhaps he was watching for him, anticipating his return and longing for fellowship with his lost son. The son came home and repented and told his father that he had sinned against heaven, and in his sight, and was not worthy to be called his son. Instead of being subjected to ridicule and rejection, he was endowed with forgiveness and favor. The disposition that the father displayed magnified the gratitude of having his son return home. When the son returned home, his father embraced him with open arms.

Perhaps oblivious to the fact that his son had disrespected him, had committed sin against both him and God, and had lost his entire inheritance, the father told his servants to bring the best robe and put it on him, and put a ring on his hand and shoes on his feet and bring the fattened calf, and kill it and let us eat and be merry. The father was not concerned with the "I told you so" or with opportunity to ridicule his son for his wayward lifestyle. The fact that his son was once lost but now was found constituted a celebration like no other.

In this parable, the return of the prodigal son to his earthly father symbolizes the penitent sinner's return to His heavenly Father. Just like the father in the parable, Jesus is waiting with open arms full of compassion for those who have lost their way and have turned away from Him. He is waiting patiently with loving compassion, ready to restore them back to His family. God longs to have fellowship with His children. The Bible says that God rejoices when a lost sinner comes home. According to St. Luke 15:7, there will be more rejoicing over one sinner than over 99 just persons that do not need to repent.

My friend, the enemy will try to torment your mind and entice you to believe that you have done too much for God to forgive you and that you have strayed to far for God to rescue you. But in the Word of God, we find that 1 John 1:9 says *If you confess our sins, he is faithful and just to forgive us our sins.* If you confess your sins before God, he can and will forgive you. Satan will try to convince you that your relationship can't be stored. But take a look at how the prodigal son went from the state of destitution to complete restoration. Psalms

103 verses 3-10 gives clear indication that a backslider can be restored back to a loving relationship with the Father.

God is merciful and loving. He is tender hearted and compassionate. Psalm 103: 3 says that he is the one forgives all of our iniquities. He redeems our life from destruction and crowns us with loving kindness and tender mercies. His mercy is great toward those that fear him. We are blessed that God does not deal with us according to our sins nor does he reward us according to our iniquities.

My plea to you is not to listen to the enemy and come back home to God where you belong. No matter what sins you have committed, no matter how long you have been away from God, he can still use you to do great things for His kingdom. Come Back Home.

Discussion Questions

1. Compare the relationship that the father had with his son and the relationship that God has with a Christian who has backslidden.

_____

_____

_____

_____

_____

_____

_____

_____

_____

_____

_____

_____

_____

_____

_____

_____

_____

_____

_____

2. How does God demonstrate his love through the parable of the prodigal son?

_____

_____

_____

_____

_____

_____

_____

_____

_____

_____

_____

_____

_____

_____

_____

_____

_____

_____

_____

_____

_____

_____

_____

RESTORING YOUR RELATIONSHIP

Chapter 10

Create in me a clean heart and renew a right spirit within me. Psalm 51:10

THE MOST IMPORTANT THING THAT you can ever do as a backslider is to restore your relationship with God. But that is the last thing that Satan would want you to do because he wants you to remain broken. He does not want you to come back to God and stand in your rightful position as a child of God. Satan wants those who have fallen away from God to live in condemnation for the sins that they have committed. Satan is well acquainted with the benefits of being in perfect harmony with Jesus Christ. After all he once had a close relationship with God. He was once in heaven and served in the position as one of God's highest ranking angels. Adorned with every jewel imaginable, he was the "anointed cherub". Ezekiel 28th chapter describes Satan as a seal of perfection, full of wisdom and perfect in beauty. He was blameless in all his ways until he allowed sin to come into his heart. Satan's sin was pride. Although he already had an exalted position, he wanted more. Isaiah 14:13, he said" I will ascend into heaven, I will exalt my throne above the stars of God. I will sit upon the mount of the congregation, in the sides of the north. I will ascend above the heights of the cloud: I will be like the most High". Satan wanted to be like God and have other angels worship him. He lost this position when he allowed pride to come in his heart which caused him to rebel against God. Because God could not allow sin to be in heaven, and because he refuses to share His praise and glory with anyone, he put Satan and the host of angels that chose to follow him out of heaven. Every since then Satan's mission has been to turn people away from God so that they will miss their destiny. He knows that you can't make it to heaven with a broken relationship with God.

Before we begin the discussion of how to restore your relationship with God, it will be essential that you have an understanding why the relationship is broken. It is broken not because of anything God has done, it is broken because of the sin that you have committed. It is all your part, not God's. God will not tolerate sin because he hates sin. He despises and he detest sin. It is an abomination in his eyesight, and it stinks in nostrils. Sin breaks the covenant terms of our relationship with God. It acts as a barrier and drives a wedge between God and us. But thank God that Jesus' death and resurrection provided the opportunity to bring restoration to the relationship between God and us.

Restoration means to bring back to original state. God is a God of restoration, he wants nothing more than to restore you back to him. He desires to see you take your rightful position as one of His obedient children and be in fellowship with Him again. You can be restored back to God only if we invite him back to be reigning King in your life. To begin the process of restoration, you must first acknowledge your sin. By acknowledging your sins, you are demonstrating that you are aware that you have sinned against God. You must become Godly sorry for the sins that you have committed.

You must also confess your sins to God. Acknowledge the fact that you have sinned and fallen short of God's glory and then confess your sins to God. To be Godly sorry goes beyond being sorry because you were caught in your sin, but it is a sincere feeling of betrayal against God in the first place.

Remember what the Israelite said to God "We have sinned against thee, both because we have forsaken our God and served Baalim." They both acknowledged and confessed their sin before God.

Once you have confessed your sins to God, the next step would be to ask God for forgiveness. I John 1:9 say "If we confess our sins, he is faithful and just to forgive us". God will forgive us, but we must be sincere when we ask him. Asking God for forgiveness helps bring a sense of peace and harmony between you and Him.

Turning away from your sin is an intricate part of the repentance process. It is not enough to just acknowledge and confess your sin, and ask for forgiveness, but you must take it a step further and turn from your sins. True repentance require sincerity and it involves action. When the Israelites were in trouble they would come to God, God would deliver them and then they would go back to their old way and ignore God. That was not true repentance because they were not genuine with God nor did they turn away from their sin. But as we have discussed earlier, the Israelites offered God a sincere confession and they turned away from their sins. Judges chapter 10:16 says "And they put away the strange gods from among them, and served the Lord and his soul was grieved for the misery of Israel.

Just as God restored Israel, he can restore you back. He will restore you back to a place of peace.

Discussion Questions

1. Discuss what makes a relationship broken between a backsliding Christian and God.

_____

_____

_____

_____

_____

_____

_____

_____

_____

_____

_____

_____

_____

_____

_____

_____

_____

_____

_____

_____

_____

2. What does the word restoration mean?

_____

_____

_____

_____

_____

_____

_____

_____

_____

_____

_____

_____

_____

_____

_____

_____

_____

_____

_____

_____

_____

_____

_____

3. How can a relationship be restored back with God? What are the steps to restoration?

_____

_____

_____

_____

_____

_____

_____

_____

_____

_____

_____

_____

_____

_____

_____

_____

_____

_____

_____

_____

_____

_____

_____

STAY ANCHORED

Chapter 11

Which hope we have as an anchor of the soul, both sure and steadfast, and which entereth into that within the veil. Hebrews 6:19

ACCORDING TO THE NEW WORLD Encyclopedia, an anchor is an object that is used to attach a ship or boat to a specific point at the bottom of a body of water. The purpose of an anchor is to stabilize the boat while docked, or secure it in the midst of a storm. Although an anchor is small compared to the size of a ship, it is powerful enough to hold the boat firm. The anchor prevents the boat or ship from drifting away caused by the action of wind and waves during a storm. In the event that a storm rises, and if the boat is not securely anchored, it will drift away.

So it is with the Christian life. We too need an anchor to hold us firm in the midst of the storm. Just like a ship, we need an anchor to stabilize us on this Christian journey. As a child of God, we have the privilege of having Jesus Christ as our anchor. Hebrews 6:19 describes him as steadfast and sure. "Which hope we have as an anchor of the soul, both sure and steadfast, and which entereth into that within the veil". We can have hope and confidence in Jesus as our anchor because he is always stable. He never changes and never moves. He is the same yesterday, today and forever (Hebrew 13:8). He is our refuge and fortress. Psalms 91:1-2 says He that dwelleth in the secret place of the Most High shall abide under the shadow of the Almighty. I will say of the Lord, He is my refuge and my fortress: my God in him will I trust. Jesus Christ is able to hold us in position so that we can't drift too far away from God. Jesus Christ is our anchor and we must stay anchored to him so when the storms come in our lives, we will not drift away. Just as the ship that is securely anchored never drifts, a life anchored to Christ will never drift.

The life of a Christian can be viewed as a ship on a sea. We, like the ship will have to endure periods of stormy weather, turbulent weather, as well as calm weather in our lives. During those times of stormy and turbulent weather, if we are not securely anchored to Jesus Christ we will drift away. This brings to my mind of a song that I once heard. The lyrics of the song say "There is a storm out on life's ocean and it is moving this away. If your soul is not anchored in Jesus, you will surely drift away". Regardless of your socioeconomic status, religion, gender or nationality, you will at some point face a storm in your life. We have trials and tribulations. In fact, Jesus tells us this in St. John 16:33 "These things I have spoken unto you, that in me ye might have peace. In the world ye shall have tribulation: but be of good cheer; I have overcome the world". Since the word of God has already forewarned us that we will face trials, and lets us know that we will have tribulations, we should not be thrown off when problems come in our lives. At least not to the point of allowing them to cause us to drift away from God. 1 Thessalonians 3:3 says "That no man should be moved (shaken) by these afflictions: for yourselves know that we are appointed thereunto". When faced with adversity, we are given the opportunity to test the stability of our anchor. If we are anchored to Jesus, then we can weather any storm. But if we are attached to anything other than Jesus, we find that our anchor does not have any stability. The problem lies in the fact that because some of us are not anchored to Jesus when trials come we find that we don't have anything to hold onto. There is not any stability in our life. We need solidity in our lives, that is why it is essential that as children of God, we stay anchored to Jesus.

So how do we stay anchored to Christ? We stay anchored to Christ by consistently abiding in him. St. John 15:4 says "Abide in me and I in you. As the branch cannot bear fruit of itself, except it abide in the vine: no more can ye, except ye abide in me". The word *abide* means "to live, continue or remain or to dwell, remain fixed in a certain place." So to abide in Christ is to live in Him or remain in Him. Abiding in Christ means having an intimate, close relationship, and not just a superficial acquaintance. Throughout this passage of scripture, Jesus used the parable of vine and branches to illustrate the closeness between us as Christians and himself. Just as the branch has to stay connected to the vine in order to gain the power for fruitfulness, we must abide in the Lord to get power to remain anchored. Jesus Christ is our power source. As long as we stay connected to our power source, we will have the ability to remain steadfast. Without this vital union between us and Christ we will be swayed and will one day wake up to find ourselves far away from the fellowship that God has provided for us in Christ Jesus.

One way of staying rooted and grounded in Christ is to stay anchored in your faith. At the time of this writing, the economy has taken a downturn. People have lost their jobs. Although this is a tough time, as Christians we should recognize that God is our source and rely on the fact that God's ability to provide for us is not dependent on the condition our economy is in. We should rest in the fact that God word is always true. So when the word says that God will supply all of our needs(Philippians 4:19), we can depend on it. But all too often, we get discouraged and allow our faith to waver. James 1:6 says "But let him ask in faith, nothing wavering, For he that wavereth is like a wave of the sea driven with the wind and tossed". In this scripture, James compares a person who doubts, or does not exhibit faith to a wave of the sea. We know that waves have high tides and low tides. It rises at a peak and then goes back down. In our Christian life, we can't ride the waves. We must be stable. James goes on to say in the eighth verse that a double minded man is unstable in all his ways. To be unstable means to lacking stability or firmness or subject to change. Being unstable in your faith is just like going on a roller coaster ride. On a roller coaster ride, you are constantly being tossed up and down and sometimes in vertical loops, so it is with your wavering faith in God. At one moment you are exercising your faith and standing on the promises of God, and the next moment you are doubting God and His ability. When we allow our emotions(feelings) to take control instead of depending on the reliability of the Word of God, that is when our faith becomes shaken or unstable.

As believers our confidence in God's Word should never change because God's Word never changes. All of God's promises are sure, so we can stand on His word. But in order to stand on God's word we must know what His word says. David knew the importance of being anchored in the word of God. He said in Psalm 119: 11 "Thy word have I hid in my heart, that I might not sin against thee. In Psalm 119:105 David said that "Thy word is a lamp unto my feet and a light unto my path". It is so important that you study and meditate on God's Word. We can stay connected to Christ when we stay anchored in the Word of God.

We all need an anchor that will keep us steady when the storms of life rage in our lives. Placing our hope and trust in a false anchor (jobs, money, relationships, success and positions) puts us in danger of sinking. But if we put our trust in the only true anchor, we can all have the testimony that though the storms sometimes rage in our lives, my soul will stay anchored in the Lord.

Discussion Questions

1. What does it mean to stay anchored in your faith?

_____

_____

_____

_____

_____

_____

_____

_____

_____

_____

_____

_____

_____

_____

_____

_____

_____

_____

_____

_____

_____

_____

2. How important is it to have Jesus Christ as your anchor?

_____

_____

_____

_____

_____

_____

_____

_____

_____

_____

_____

_____

_____

_____

_____

_____

_____

_____

_____

_____

_____

_____

_____

_____

HOW TO HELP RESTORE A DRIFTING BELIEVER

Chapter 12

Brethren, if a man be overtaken in a fault, you who are spiritual, restore such a one in the spirit of meekness; considering yourself, lest you also be tempted. Galatians 6:1

THE WORD OF GOD TEACHES us that as believers we have a responsibility to those who have strayed away from God's truth and His ways. As faithful believers, we must help draw our erring brother or sister back to fellowship with the Lord. Galatians 6:1 says "Brethren, if a man be overtaken in a fault, ye which are spiritual, restore such an one in the spirit of meekness: considering thyself, lest thou also be tempted". This scripture gives clear instructions on how we are to handle a brother or sister who has fallen back into sin.

First it is important to note that these instructions are addressed to the spiritually mature. To be spiritually mature means to be constantly walking in the spirit and living by the spirit and exhibiting the fruit of the spirit in your life. The spiritually mature are the ones who should restore their brother or sister back to Christ. Restoring a sinning brother or sister must be done in the spirit of meekness. Meekness is one of the fruit of the spirit. It is the opposite of arrogance and harshness. We must never speak or act out of judgment or condemnation.

This passage of scripture also gives us a warning when it comes to restoring our brother or sister. It says "considering yourself, lest you also be tempted". None of us are exempt from temptation. That is why we must pay careful attention and watch out for ourselves as we help restore our brother or sister who has strayed away from God. If we are not on guard, we might very well fall into temptation ourselves. It is similar to the case of a person trying to save a drowning victim. I am sure we have all heard of a story or two about how a heroic person drowns only after trying to save someone else life. Imagine this; you and your friend have decided to spend a nice relaxing day at the beach. Your friends who are all avid swimmers and very adventurous they decide to go out into the deepest part of the water at the beach, while you remain in the shallow part. After a couple of minutes, you notice that one of your friends is in danger. You start to panic as you see her head bob up and down under the water a couple of times. She is going under. You decide that you are going to try to save her, so you run divide into the water as swim as best as you can. You get to your friend and try to bring her back to shore. She is fighting so hard against the water, that it makes it difficult to help her. She evidently pulls you under the water, and now both of you need to be rescued.

Although you meant well and you really wanted to help your friend, would it had be a better choice to let someone who has more expertise in saving someone who is drowning than to trying to help your friend? The same applies spiritually. If you are not spiritually mature enough to restore your brother or sister back to Christ without falling into temptation, it is best that you not engage in that battle. Now am I saying that you should not try to help at all? I most certainly am not, but what I am saying is that if you are not strong enough in your spiritual walk, to help pull someone back to "shore" and into their rightful position in God without falling into temptation, then let someone else help that person. At the same time, your spiritual immature is not to be used as an excuse for not helping lead a lost soul back to restoration to God. Eventually God expects you to grow up into a mature Christian.

1Peter 2:2 says "As newborn babes, desire the sincere milk of the word that ye may grow thereby: If so be ye have tasted that the Lord is gracious". Ephesians 4:14-15 says "That we henceforth be no more children, tossed to and fro and carried about with every wind of doctrine, by the sleight of men, cunning craftiness, whereby they lie in wait to deceive; 15.But speaking the truth in love, may grow up into him in all things, which is the head, even Christ."

Although it is our responsibility, many Christians don't take this responsibility serious enough. This is very evident as we take at look at the dysfunctional families, divorce rate and high crime rate. Some Christians don't attempt to lead their brother or sister back to Christ for a number of reasons. One reason that Christians are often hesitant to confront a sinning brother or sister is because they know that there is sin in their own lives. They are aware of their own shortcomings and don't want to appear as a hypocrite. Some Christians would rather avoid having confrontations with the Christian who has turned away from God. They don't want to be judgmental or critical. Then there are some who think that it would all be in vain to help the person because they would fall into sin again.

But the truth of the matter is that regardless of what reason that you and I may have we are still required to help. We can't ignore the fact that our brother or sister has fallen into sin. We must exert bold faith to engage in spiritual warfare against the forces of darkness to break the chains of bondage and confront the sin which our backsliding brother or sister has become entangled in. We must be willing to help our brother or sister even if they don't see the need to be rescued.

We can't sit back and watch our fellow sisters and brothers shipwreck their lives. To do that would be just like a watching a child run into a busy street in front a car and you not saying anything to stop him or her. We are applying the same concept if we don't say anything to someone who has strayed from God. Sometimes instead of trying to convince the person to turn back to God, often times we gossip about the person. You might not be guilty of being the gossiper, but I am sure you know someone who does gossip. You know how they do, they get on the telephone or they text on their cell phone, or some are even bold enough to send messages on the internet and tell the latest gossip that they have heard about a person. I've heard people say "Now I'm telling you this so you will be aware of what is going on and you can be praying about it". I personally think that they use this technique so they can cover up the fact that they are gossiping, which by the way is a sin. Spreading the word about the person does not help, it only causes more damage.

Instead of gossiping about the person who has turned away from God, we should stand in the gap and display a love that covers sin. Proverbs 10:12 says *"Hatred stirreth up strifes: but love covers a multitude of sins"*. That is to say that we are not to condone the sin, but we are to treat the person with love. The story of Noah and his three sons, Ham. Shem and Japheth depict the concept of covering someone in love, instead of exposing the sin. Noah had become drunk and laid uncovered in his tent. Ham saw his father in this condition, and went out to tell his brothers. Ham spread the word about Noah instead of covering his father up. Shem and Japheth took a different approach. They got a garment and walked in backwards to cover their father so they would not see him naked. Shem and Japheth demonstrated an act of love. This is the type example God wants us to follow.

The Word of God gives further instructions concerning our brothers and sisters who have fallen into sin. Apostle John tells us in 1John 5: 16 that" if any man see his brother sin a sin which is not unto death, he shall ask, and he shall give him life for them that sin not unto death. There is a sin unto death: I do not say that he shall pray for it". Verse 17 says "All unrighteousness is sin: and there is a sin not unto death. In this passage of scripture, John divides all sins into two categories: sins that lead to death and sins that do not lead to death. John tells us we should pray for those whose sins do not lead to death. If we see our brother commit a sin that does not lead to death, that we should pray and ask God to give him life. We should intercede on behalf of our brother but only if the sin does not lead to death. However, for those whose sins lead to death, we are not to pray on their behalf. The mention of death in these two passages of scripture is referring to a spiritual death. Paul tells us in Romans 6:23 *"For the wages of sin is death: but the gift of God is eternal life through Jesus Christ our Lord"*. Not every sin that we commit will lead us to death. It is when we fail to repent of our sins, and continue to willfully sin against God and the Holy Ghost, that we are in danger of a spiritual death. Jesus makes it very clear that blaspheming against the Holy Ghost is a sin cannot be forgiven. Mark 3:28-29 says *"Verily I say unto you, all sins shall be forgiven unto the sons of men, and blasphemies wherewith soever they shall blaspheme. But he that shall blaspheme against the Holy Ghost hath never forgiveness; but is in danger of eternal damnation."*

Hebrews 10:26-27 says *"For if we willfully after that we have received the knowledge of the truth, there remaineth no more sacrifice of sins. 27. But for a certain fearful looking for of judgment and fiery indignation, which shall devour the adversaries.* If a believer continues to willfully sin and refuses to repent, it is impossible to bring back to God. Sometimes a person has gone too far in their sins that it does not serve a purpose in praying for them. God will not listen to the prayers on their behalf. A good example of that is found in Jeremiah 7:16 *"Therefore pray not thou for this people, neither lift up cry nor prayer for them, neither make intercession to me: for I will not hear thee".* It had reached a point in that Judah had sinned against God that he instructed Jeremiah not to pray for the nation because he was not going to listen to the prayers on their behalf. Their only option was death.

It is not God's desire that any one perishes. He wants everyone to be saved. 2 Peter 3:9 says, *"The Lord is not slack concerning his promises, as some men count slackness; but is longsuffering to usward, not willing that any should perish, but that all should come to repentance".*

My sisters and my brothers, time is drawing near. While we still have time and while there is still hope, let us intercede on behalf of our penitent brothers and sisters. Maybe you know a family member, an acquaintance, a friend or a church member who has drifted away from God. They once walked close to Jesus and but now have strayed far away from Him. We all know people who were once full of love for the Lord but for some reason or another God is no longer a part of their lives.

My friend it is our responsibility to go to battle for our fallen brother. We can't be too passive or too hesitant about snatching our fellow man from the clutches of the enemy. We must remain committed to those who have strayed away from the truth and lost their connection with God, and strive to help them reach a turning point in their lives and be restored back to God.

Restoring a sinning brother requires both humility and faith. Abraham demonstrated both faith and humility when his nephew decided to move his tents toward Sodom. This decision put Lot in a position which caused him to have a spiritual downfall in which he never recovered.

Discussion Questions

What Would You Do?

1. Suppose you were confronted with dealing with a couple who have turned away from God. They once were in church serving God faithfully, but now they are living life like as unbelievers. What would you do?

Option#1—Would you simply look away and do nothing?
Option #2—Would you spread the word about the couple to anybody who will listen about the sins that the erring couple has committed?
Option #3—Would you show love and help the couple turn back to God?

I pray that you chose option #3 because when you cover another believer's sin, you are in the position to receive God's mercy to cover your sins. James 2:13 says *For he shall have judgment without mercy, that hath showed no mercy; and mercy rejoiceth against judgement.*

2. How can you help restore your erring brother or sister back to Christ?

_____

_____

_____

_____

_____

_____

_____

_____

_____

_____

_____

_____

_____

_____

_____

_____

_____

_____

_____

_____

_____

_____

3. What are some barriers or excuses which keep some Christians from attempting to restore a Christian who has turned away from God?

_____

_____

_____

_____

_____

_____

_____

_____

_____

_____

_____

_____

_____

_____

_____

_____

_____

_____

_____

_____

_____

Intercessory Prayer for the Backslider

Lord, I come to you interceding on behalf of those who have strayed away from you. I ask that you send your Holy Spirit to convict them and draw them back to you. Father allow your cleansing blood to flow through their hardened hearts and give them new life in their hearts. Restore their sensitivity to sin and help them to see sin as you see it. Let them despise the things that you despise and love the things that you love. Give them the courage to crucify them flesh and die to themselves. I pray for complete transformation that those areas that led them away from you will be purified. Father create a clean heart within them so that they will not sin against you. Give them the strength to recommit themselves to you and walk in total obedience to you. Release them from the bondage of sin. As they resurrender Lordship of their lives to you, fill them with the Holy Spirit and take full control over their lives. Lead them and guide them in the will and plan that you have for their lives. Restore the joy of their salvation.

Scriptures on Backsliding

1.) **Kings 11:9** And the LORD was angry with Solomon, because his heart was turned from the LORD God of Israel, which had appeared unto him twice.

2.) **Galatians 3:1-3** "You foolish Galatians! Who has bewitched you? Before your very eyes Jesus Christ was clearly portrayed as crucified. I would like to learn just one thing from you: Did you receive the Spirit by observing the law, or by believing what you heard? Are you so foolish? After beginning with the Spirit, are you now trying to attain your goal by human effort?" (NIV)

3.) **Revelation 2:4** "Nevertheless I have somewhat against thee, because thou hast left thy first love."

4.) **Isaiah 59:2** But your iniquities have separated between you and your God, and your sins have hid his face from you, that he will not hear.

5.) **Galatians 5:4-7** You who are trying to be justified by law have been alienated from Christ; you have fallen away from grace. But by faith we eagerly await through the Spirit the righteousness for which we hope. For in Christ Jesus neither circumcision nor uncircumcision has any value. The only thing that counts is faith expressing itself through love. You were running a good race. Who cut in on you and kept you from obeying the truth? (NIV)

6.) **Exodus 32:8** They have turned aside quickly out of the way which I commanded them: they have made them a molten calf, and have worshipped it, and have sacrificed thereunto, and said, These be thy gods, O Israel, which have brought thee up out of the land of Egypt.

7.) **Jeremiah 3:12** Go and proclaim these words toward the north, and say, Return, thou backsliding Israel, saith the LORD; and I will not cause mine anger to fall upon you: for I am merciful, saith the LORD, and I will not keep anger forever.

8). **Jeremiah 3:22** Return, ye backsliding children, and I will heal your backslidings. Behold, we come unto thee; for thou art the LORD our God.

9.) **Jeremiah 3:13** Only acknowledge thine iniquity, that thou hast transgressed against the LORD thy God, and hast scattered thy ways to the strangers under every green tree, and ye have not obeyed my voice, saith the LORD.

10.) **Jeremiah 31:20** Is Ephraim my dear son? is he a pleasant child? for since I spake against him, I do earnestly remember him still: therefore my bowels are troubled for him; I will surely have mercy upon him, saith the LORD.

11.) **Psalms 51:1** Have mercy upon me, O God, according to thy lovingkindness: according unto the multitude of thy tender mercies blot out my transgressions.

12.) **Psalms 51:10**—Create in me a clean heart, O God, and renew a right spirit within me.

13.) **Psalms 6:4** Return, O LORD, deliver my soul: oh save me for thy mercies' sake.

14.) **Joel 2:13** And rend your heart, and not your garments, and turn unto the LORD your God: for he is gracious and merciful, slow to anger, and of great kindness, and repenteth him of the evil.

15.) **Psalms 32:5** I acknowledged my sin unto thee, and mine iniquity have I not hid. I said, I will confess my transgressions unto the LORD; and thou forgavest the iniquity of my sin. Selah.

16.) **Proverbs 28:13** He that covereth his sins shall not prosper: but whoso confesseth and forsaketh them shall have mercy.

17.) **Proverbs 28:14** Happy is the man that feareth alway: but he that hardeneth his heart shall fall into mischief.

18.) **Isaiah 26:3-4** Thou wilt keep him in perfect peace, whose mind is stayed on thee: because he trusteth in thee. Trust ye in the LORD for ever: for in the LORD JEHOVAH is everlasting strength:

19.) **Jeremiah 3:14** Turn, O backsliding children, saith the LORD; for I am married unto you: and I will take you one of a city, and two of a family, and I will bring you to Zion:

20.) **Jeremiah 3:22** Return, ye backsliding children, and I will heal your backslidings. Behold, we come unto thee; for thou art the LORD our God.

21.) **Isaiah 55:7** Let the wicked forsake his way, and the unrighteous man his thoughts: and let him return unto the LORD, and he will have mercy upon him; and to our God, for he will abundantly pardon.

22.) **Luke 15:18-20** I will arise and go to my father, and will say unto him, Father, I have sinned against heaven, and before thee, And am no more worthy to be called thy son: make me as one of thy hired servants. And he arose, and came to his father. But when he was yet a great way off, his father saw him, and had compassion, and ran, and fell on his neck, and kissed him.

23.) Jeremiah 14:7-9 "Although our sins testify against us, O LORD, do something for the sake of your name. For our backsliding is great; we have sinned against you. O Hope of Israel, its Savior in times of distress, why are you like a stranger in the land, like a traveler who stays only a night? Why are you like a man taken by surprise, like a warrior powerless to save? You are among us, O LORD, and we bear your name; do not forsake us!" (NIV)

24.) Hosea 14:4 I will heal their backsliding, I will love them freely: for mine anger is turned away from him.

25.) Psalms 130:7 Let Israel hope in the LORD: for with the LORD there is mercy, and with him is plenteous redemption.

26.) 1 Corinthians 10:12 Wherefore let him that thinketh he standeth take heed lest he fall.

27.) Psalm 51

Have mercy upon me, O God, according to thy loving kindness: according unto the multitude of thy tender mercies blot out my transgressions. Wash me throughly from mine iniquity, and cleanse me from my sin. For I acknowledge my transgressions: and my sin is ever before me.

Against thee, thee only, have I sinned, and done this evil in thy sight: that thou mightest be justified when thou speakest, and be clear when thou judgest. Behold, I was shapen in iniquity; and in sin did my mother conceive me. Behold, thou desirest truth in the inward parts: and in the hidden part thou shalt make me to know wisdom.

Purge me with hyssop, and I shall be clean: wash me, and I shall be whiter than snow. Make me to hear joy and gladness; that the bones which thou hast broken may rejoice. Hide thy face from my sins, and blot out all mine iniquities. Create in me a clean heart, O God; and renew a right spirit within me.

Cast me not away from thy presence; and take not thy holy spirit from me. Restore unto me the joy of thy salvation; and uphold me with thy free spirit.

Then will I teach transgressors thy ways; and sinners shall be converted unto thee. Deliver me from bloodguiltiness, O God, thou God of my salvation: and my tongue shall sing aloud of thy righteousness. O Lord, open thou my lips; and my mouth shall shew forth thy praise. For thou desirest not sacrifice; else would I give it: thou delightest not in burnt offering. The sacrifices of God are a broken spirit: a broken and a contrite heart, O God, thou wilt not despise.

Do good in thy good pleasure unto Zion: build thou the walls of Jerusalem. Then shalt thou be pleased with the sacrifices of righteousness, with burnt offering and whole burnt offering: then shall they offer bullocks upon thine altar.

28.) Psalms 80:3 Turn us again, O God, and cause thy face to shine; and we shall be saved.

29.) Psalms 85:4 Turn us, O God of our salvation, and cause thine anger toward us to cease.

30.) Lamentations 5:21 Turn thou us unto thee, O LORD, and we shall be turned; renew our days as of old.

31.) 2 Chronicles 7:14 If my people, which are called by my name, shall humble themselves, and pray, and seek my face, and turn from their wicked ways; then will I hear from heaven, and will forgive their sin, and will heal their land.

32.) Psalms 37:24 Though he fall, he shall not be utterly cast down: for the LORD upholdeth him with his hand.

33.) Proverbs 24:16 For a just man falleth seven times, and riseth up again: but the wicked shall fall into mischief.

34.) **Hosea 14:4** I will heal their backsliding, I will love them freely: for mine anger is turned away from him.

35.) **Psalms 147:11** The LORD taketh pleasure in them that fear him, in those that hope in his mercy.

36.) **Psalms 85:8** I will hear what God the LORD will speak: for he will speak peace unto his people, and to his saints: but let them not turn again to folly.